Is The Qur'an God's Word?

A Scientific Approach

SAMI ASHOURI, MD

amana publications

Contents

Introduction 7

Preface 11

Chapter 1: The Universe: Landmarks of the Creation 13

Chapter 2: The Heavens and the Earth: Stages of the Creation...... 21

Chapter 3: Ascension in the Sky 31

Chapter 4: The Lowest Earth 35

Chapter 5: The Descended Iron 43

Chapter 6: Mountains are Pegs 49

Chapter 7: Human Reproduction 53

Chapter 8: Water in the Living Organism 59

Chapter 9: Qur'anic Comments on the Honeybee 61

Chapter 10: The Existence of Sex in Plants 69

Chapter 11: Rainfall 77

Chapter 12: Where the Seas Meet 83

Chapter 13: Two More Observations 93

The Qur'anic Verses in Arabic Language 95

Introduction

In order for the non-Muslim reader to clearly understand the Qur'anic verses cited in this book, it is essential to know that Islamic ideology is based on the concept that the Qur'an is the word of God. This does not simply mean an "inspiration" from God but means the very word which God had actually spoken and conveyed to Muhammad through the angel Gabriele. When God expresses Himself in the Qur'an, He sometimes refers to Himself as "**I**" and frequently as "**We**" for greatness and distinction from mankind, although the pronoun "**We**" implies only God Himself. At times, He presents His preaching as a third party using the pronoun "He" or the term "the one **Who**." We should mention here that the word "Allah" is simply the Arabic translation of the word "God", and is the word used in the Arabic version of the Bible when referring to God. Repeatedly, the Qur'an affirms that God of Islam is the same God of Christianity, Judaism and all past prophets.

It is evident that the Qur'an is not a book of science but a book of preaching to mankind. During the context of preaching, many reflections were presented on elements of the Creation and various natural phenomena in order to express the greatness of God and His sovereignty over the universe. "A scientific approach" to the Qur'an is a scientific review and examination of these statements made in the Qur'an which were found, many centuries later, with the advent of modern science, to conform to modern scientific discoveries.

It is essential to mention here that the Qur'an affirms that the Bible, in its original form, is also the word of God and refers to it as "the book." It is composed of two separate books, both of which were revealed by God, namely the Torah which has been revealed to Moses and the Gospel which has been revealed to Jesus Christ. Therefore, many passages or narrations in the Bible and the Qur'an might be similar or identical. Some passages might show some variation from the Bible's version while others might be completely new and nonexistent in the Bible.

Islamic theology maintains that Muhammad is the prophet referred to by Moses in the Bible, when making the statement to his people that "The Lord your God will raise up for you a prophet, like me, from your midst, from your brethren (meaning Ishmael) him you shall hear" [Deuteronomy 18:5–15] & "I...will put My words in his mouth" (meaning the Qur'an) [Deuteronomy 18:5–18].

Christian teaching assumes that the prophecy made by Moses actually referred to Jesus Christ. Muslims see it as a reference to Muhammad based on the substantial similarity between Moses and Muhammad. This included an orphan childhood, receiving their first command from God while on a mountain with Moses being on Mount Sinai while Muhammad being on Mount Hira, exodus to another land with Moses exiting to "Madian" and Muhammad exiting to "Medina", and engaging into battles to defend their faith and their people. Muslims see no resemblance of Jesus Christ to Moses. According to the Qur'an, Jesus was sent as "a miracle to mankind and a mercy from God" [the Qur'an; 19 –21]. He was also "the prophet of God, and His word which He released to Mary, and a soul from Him" [the Qur'an; 4 –171]. Unlike any other prophet, he had a miraculous birth to Mary the virgin [the Qur'an; Surah 19], and was lifted to heavens after his death as God had addressed him "I am raising you up to me" [the Qur'an; 3–55]. Although not clearly expressed in the Qur'an, two of Muhammad statements indicate that Jesus Christ would return near the end of time to prevail over his enemies.

In spite of this position the Qur'an assigns to Jesus Christ, there is a distinct difference between Islam and Christianity in that Islam does not consider Jesus Christ son of God and does not approve the trinity concept, simply because associating anyone with God is degrading to Him, who, alone, holds the dominion over the entire universe. According to the Qur'an, all the miracles Jesus Christ performed were made possible only through a specific inspiration from God and through God's support to him by the holy spirit. In this sense, the Qur'an affirms that Islam is the universal message God had presented to mankind, along the ages, to worship and submit to one God. Islam specific meaning is "submission to God."

Muhammad, according to Islam, was the last messenger of God and the "seal of the prophets." He was presumably unlettered who did not write or read. When a chapter or a passage of the Qur'an was revealed to him, he recited it to his scribes and followers who recorded it on various writing materials available at the time. Therefore, written copy of the revelations were maintained with his scribes and followers during his lifetime. The Qur'anic revelations, shortly after Muhammad's death, were combined into a single book under the supervision of his closest scribe Zeid who was known as "the scribe of the prophet." That single copy of the book was adopted as the only official copy which has been transmitted, unaltered, till the present time. For details of the process of collecting the Qur'an and its authenticity, please refer to Dr. Maurice Bucaille's book, *The Qur'an the Bible and Science* [pp. 133 to 138].

The Qur'an was revealed in successive passages over a period of 23 years beginning in 610 A.D. when Muhammad turned forty and ending in 632 A.D. with the time of his death. Knowing and remembering these dates is essential to understanding the chronology of the scientific knowledge that evolved since the Qur'an was revealed up to modern times.

As the Qur'anic revelations were combined in a single book, the statements Muhammad made during his daily living events and when facing special situations as well as his own breaching of mankind were subsequently compiled ,shortly after his death, as "statements of the prophet" or "Hadith." During his lifetime, Muhammad prohibited his followers from writing down his own statements for the concern they might be mingled with the Qur'anic revelations. He, however, issued a sound warning to his companions and the generations to come that "whosoever attributed to me something I had not said, he shall reserve his seat in hellfire."

The only other publication in English, which I am aware of, which deals with the subject of science in the Qur'an, in a scientific fashion, is Dr. Maurice Bucaille's book titled *The Bible the Qur'an and Science* which has originally been translated from French by Dr. Bucaille himself. Limited and less involved publications also exist in Arabic. This book is an examination of the subject in some details with emphasis on the chronology of scientific knowledge which might be helpful to the reader to answer the question: "Is the Qur'an God's word?"

Preface

The quotation of the Qur'anic verses throughout this book is given in brackets beginning with the number of the Surah and followed by the number of the verse within that Surah. The quotation of references is also given in brackets and begins with the number of the reference (cited at the end of each chapter) followed by the relevant number of the page referenced.

For easy referencing, the Qur'anic verses cited in this book are listed chapterwise in their original Arabic form in a separate section. The grouping of these verses in Arabic follows the sequence of their corresponding English translation appearing in each chapter of the book.

The English translation of the Arabic text was mainly accessed from Abdullah Yusuf 'Ali's translation of the Qur'an, which is the most commonly used translation and commentary in the West. Abdullah Yusuf 'Ali, who was born in India in 1872, is said to have memorized the entire Qur'an by heart at an early age. He had a firm command of both, the Arabic language which he began learning in childhood, and the English language which he studied in London over many years. The first edition of his English translation and commentary was published in 1934.

Because the translation was crafted mostly in theological style, I preferred, on several occasions, a literal translation of some words to ensure that the exact Arabic meaning is being delivered in English. For this literal translation of some words or expressions, I have used *The Arabic-English Dictionary* [Al Mawred Al Quareeb, *An Arabic-English Dictionary* by Dr Rohi Baalbaki. Dar El Elm Lilmalayin, 2001] and *The Arabic-Arabic Dictionary* [Mukhtar Al Sihah, *An Arabic-Arabic Dictionary* by Al Razi. Al Mustakbal.]

1

The Universe
Landmarks of the Creation

THE BIG BANG EXPLOSION AND FORMATION OF THE GALAXIES AND STARS

THE BELGIAN ASTRONOMER Georges Lemaitre, in 1927, addressing the origin of the universe, proposed that the entire universe was once condensed into a single mass which subsequently exploded. This extremely condensed mass which contained all the matter in the universe was called the primeval atom and the massive explosion was called the "big bang" explosion [1-55 & 4-6]. Evidence to confirm the Big Bang theory accumulated in 1965, when the American radio astronomers Arno Penzias and Robert Wilson discovered microwave signals which were transmitted from every direction in the sky which meant the universe is saturated with electromagnetic radiation [2–218]. This was later recognized as an echo of the big bang explosion, and this discovery has been supported by numerous experiments including satellite experiments [2–219].

The material which resulted after the big bang explosion was described by Parker as "a blinding white fog" which we could not see through and this grew into "thin gas in an inky black background" [1-98 & 97]. This materiel was also called the stellar gas cloud, the enormous gas cloud or simply the gas clouds. Subsequently, there was fluctuation in density of this gas with some areas becoming more dense and appearing as clumps. After progressive cooling, and in a manner which Parker compared to transformation of steam into water and subsequently into ice upon gradual cooling, the condensation of this gas at the more dense locations, or clumps, led to the birth of galaxies in these areas [1 - 94 & 4 - 7]. Stars form inside every galaxy, that each galaxy contains billions of stars. It is important to note that the formation of the galaxies and stars has been a continuous and ongoing process which began shortly after the big bang and continued for billions of years up to modern times [2–39].

The Qur'an describes the beginning of the Creation by the following statement "Do not the unbelievers realize that the heavens and Earth were joined together then we clove them asunder" [Surah 21: Verse 30]. Although the Earth belongs to our solar system which formed several billion years after the big bang, as we would see in the next chapter, our solar system, including the Earth, formed from the same enormous gas clouds which resulted from the big bang explosion.

With respect to the state of gas that existed prior to and during formation of the galaxies and stars, the Qur'an makes the following statement "and God tended to the sky and it was smoke. He said to it and to the Earth: come you willingly or unwillingly. They said we do come in willing obedience" [Surah 41: Verse 11]. The words "come you " are likely meant to command the Earth and the sky to a conjunctive function (working together) which would be required for future propagation of life on Earth, and the words "willingly or unwillingly" are meant to express the decisive command of God. Compare the Qur'anic word "smoke " to Parker's own words, when describing the state of gas in the universe, as "a blinding white fog" and "thin gas in an inky black background" [1– 97 & 98].

EXPANSION OF THE UNIVERSE

Sometime after the big bang explosion, galaxies began moving away from each other or, as scientifically stated, "the universe began expanding." This discovery was first made by Edwin Hubbell who, in 1929, along with Milton Humason ,determined the speed of movement of several dozen galaxies and their distance from us and formulated what is known as "Hubble's Law" [3-135]. Hubble's law indicates that galaxies are moving away from us at speed directly proportional to their distance from us ,so the farther away the galaxy is the faster it is receding from us [3–135]. Generally speaking, galaxies are not moving away only from us but away from each other, which leads to the conclusion that the entire universe is expanding [3–57].

The Qur'an addresses this concept with the following statement "and the sky, We constructed it firmly, and We are expanding it" [Surah 51: Verse 47]. This verse, first affirms that the sky or the universe has been constructed. Such, the steady state theory of the universe existence pioneered by Bondi, Gold, and Hoyle in 1948 [4–8] is rejected. This had become a scientific fact since Penzias and Wilson discovered the echoes of the big bang in 1965 [2–218]. The steady state universe theory originally proposed that the universe had always existed in its present state having no beginning and no end [1–153]. We should mention here that the idea of "creating" is not unique to the Qur'an and is of course shared with other religious books, as it is a religious idea. To the contrary, the steady state universe is philosophically an atheist idea. Secondly, this Qur'anic statement specifies that the construction occurred firmly, which likely refers to the gravitational forces which firmly connects the various structures of the universe. The last part of this statement clearly defines the universe as expanding.

CURVING OF SPACE

When objects move or light rays travel through the universe, they do not travel in a straight path but they follow the curvature of space created by nearby masses [3–126]. The presence of matter throughout the universe produces gravity effect on such traveling objects or light causing a warped path [5–242]. Halpern explained how the extent of curving in a particular region of space depend on its content of matter, therefore, the greater the mass in a given region, the greater curving it produces. The sun, for example, as a massive body, distorts the path of nearby objects ,such as the planets and asteroids, causing a bowl- like path [5-242 & 243]. In extreme cases when gravity is so intense by the presence of masses much larger and more dense than our sun, space is so tightly curved and light cannot even escape and does not reach us, so such places are called "black holes"[3–127].

One Qur'anic verse makes the following statement "if We opened to them a door in the sky and they were to rise lamely through it" [Surah 15: Verse 14]. In another verse, the Qur'an states "the angels and the spirit curve to Him in a day which measures fifty thousand years" [Surah 70: Verse 4]. The reader need not concern himself or herself with the specific issues addressed in these two verses because this is beyond the subject of discussion. The intended purpose here is to show that when the Qur'an refers to "rising in the sky," it refers to it as occurring in a limping or curving fashion. *The Arabic-English Dictionary* translates the word "*Araja*" as "walk lamely or walk in lameness or to limp" [6 –274]. *The Arabic- Arabic Dictionary* explains the word "*Inaraja*" as "curves" and the word "*Munaraj*" as "curving to the right and to the left" [7-- 372]. These words, in Arabic, are the same as the words used in these two Qur'anic verses or are past or present verbs or adjectives of these words.

THE FATE OF OUR UNIVERSE

With the continuous expansion of our universe, the question comes up as to what is the fate of all this?. Scientists had two theories to explain the possible end of the universe. This would depend on whether the universe is closed "finite" or open "infinite." A finite universe would "curve back on itself, like the surface of the earth, so that voyagers moving into a straight line eventually find themselves back at their starting point"[8–86], or as Dauber and Muller described it, a closed universe would "fold back on itself" [3–174] or the expansion would cease and the universe will collapse back on itself to form what is called a "big crunch" [4–208]. In a closed universe model, a "big crunch" can contain all the matter and energy in the universe and would be capable of exploding all over again into a new " big bang" [4–209]. An open universe would continue to expand and slowly fade trillions and trillions of years into the future [5–262] or as the number of years is more representatively expressed by Thuan that "to write out such a number I would have to follow the figure 1 with as many zeroes that there are hydrogen atoms in all the hundreds of billions of galaxies in the observable universe" [4–210].

In order for scientists to determine whether the universe is open or closed, they examine two factors believed to influence this outcome. One factor is the "rate of expansion" of the universe and the other is the "density" of the universe.

New observations published in 1998 suggested that the universe expansion is continuing and not slowing enough to allow "closing of the universe" and could rather be slightly accelerating [5–261]. Therefore, some scientists readily began to advocate the "open" universe model [9 –187]. Richard Morris, for multiple reasons he listed, thought that the findings are "not totally conclusive" [10 –67].

Others related that although the expansion is not slowing now but this does not mean slowing and subsequent closing would not occur in the future [4–208]. Malone, in 2001, noted that the closed universe, advocated by the American physicist John Wheeler and others, had perfectly sound mathematics [4–209].

Another factor appears to be essential in making the conclusion is the "density" of the universe, which is the concentration of matter within a specific volume. For an open universe model, the density should be less than three electrons per cubic meter and the present estimates ranges from one tenth to 10 times this critical value [10–61]. A high density would, with passage of time, leads to gradual closing of the universe due to the effect of greater gravitational forces finally leading to a reversal of the" big bang" process into a "big crunch." Some scientists think the present estimates of the density of the universe is not high enough to cause closing of the universe [5–255]. Such conclusion cannot be made with certainty because what is normally measured is the mass of the galaxies or the material which emit light so it becomes visible to us. There is large invisible matter within a given galaxy, among the galaxies and in the vast regions of the universe known as "dark matter" because it does not emit light and can not be measured [5–257]. It is estimated that at least 90 percent and perhaps as much as 99 percent of the mass of the universe is in the form of invisible or dark matter [10–59]. Richard Morris related that "since no one knows how much dark matter is there, it is impossible to calculate whether the universe is open, closed or near the borderline" [10–59]. Halpern indicated that knowing a more complete picture of the "dark matter" over the coming decades will help determining whether the universe is open or closed [5–259].

For scientists who are proponents of the closed universe model, and those who believe that creation and demise of the universe is a recurring cycle (at least for one more cycle), the Qur'an, fourteen hundred years ago, lent support to them with a decisive statement "the day will come when We will fold the heavens like a scroll is folded over a book. As We initiated the first creation, so We shall repeat it, a promise from us truly We shall fulfill" [Surah 21: Verse 104].

This verse affirms that our universe does have an end, therefore, scientifically would be finite. It describes the manner by which the universe will end as the heavens would be "folded." Compare the Qur'anic word "fold "to the words Dauber and Muller used in describing the closed universe model "fold back on itself" [3-174]. It also promises that a new universe will be recreated in a manner similar to the original creation of the present universe, which is in agreement with what John Wheeler and other scientists firmly advocate [4 -209].

REFERENCES

1. Parker, Barry. *Creation: The Story of the Origin and Evolution of the Universe*. Plenum Press. New York, 1988.

2. Fritzsch, Harald. *The Creation of Matter: The Universe from Beginning to End*. Basic Books. New York,1984.

3. Dauber, Phillip M, Muller Richard A. *The Three Big Bangs: Comet Crashes, Exploding Stars, and the Creation of the Universe*. Perseus Books. Cambridge, M.A., 1996.

4. Malone, John Williams. *Unsolved Mysteries of Science*. John Wiley & Sons, Inc. New York, 2001.

5. Halpern, Paul. *Countdown to Apocalypse: A Scientific Exploration of the End of the World.* Perseus Books. Cambridge, M.A.,2000.

6. Baalbaki, Rohi. *Al-Mawrid Al-Quareeb. A Pocket Arabic--English Dictionary.* Dar El-Ilm Lilmalayin. Beirut- Lebanon, 1991.

7. Al Razi. Mukhtar Al Sihah, *An Arabic--Arabic Dictionary. Al Mustakbal.*

8. Goldsmith, Donald. *Astronomers.* St. Martin's press. New York, 1991.

9, Odenwald, Sten F. *Back to the Astronomy Cafe.* Perseus Books Group, Boulder CO, 2003.

10. Morris, Richard. *The Universe, the Eleventh Dimension, and Everything: What we know and how we knew it.* Four Walls Eight Windows. New York, 1999.

2

The Heavens & the Earth
Stages of the Creation

THE CREATION OF the Heavens and the Earth is described, in several passages, in the Qur'an as having occurred in six days. The definition of "day" in the Qur'an implies "a period of time" or "stage", as we would see below. Unlike the prevalent concept that God rested on the 7th day, the Qur'an denies that God had become tired or that He rested after the Creation was completed "and no weariness had touched Us " [Surah 50: Verse 38].

The Qur'an entails that the meaning of "day" to humans does not have the same meaning elsewhere. In one verse the Qur'an describes a "day" as being equal to one thousand years of what humans calculates" verily a day in the sight of your Lord is like a thousand years of your reckoning " [Surah 22: Verse 47]. In another verse ,the Qur'an describes a "day" as being equal to fifty thousand years "the angels and the spirit ascend to Him in a day which measures fifty thousand years" [Surah 70: Verse 4]. The meaning of the word "day" as "stage" or "period of time" is the meaning assumed by modern Qur'anic commentaries. A similar meaning was noted, according to Dr. Bucaille, by some Qur'anic commentators as early as the 16th century [1–141]. The exact length of stages of the Creation, as many Qur'anic commentators indicated, remains largely unknown.

As Dr. Bucaille previously related, the Qur'an does not lay a precise sequence for stages of the Creation [1–143]. There are numerous verses throughout the book which refer to various aspects of the Creation. Many verses contain simple reflections and are intended to draw the attention of mankind to uniqueness of God's creations, as God is the Creator, Designer and Commander of the Heavens and Earth. There are three passages, which comment on stages of the Creation, that we would address here.. As each passage contains multiple verses, and for the purpose of easy referencing, we would designate these groups of verses as passages No. 1, No. 2 and No. 3. We should mention here that the Arabic language does not differentiate between the words "heavens" and "sky", therefore, these words might be used interchangeably in English, although the word "Heavens" is commonly used as a translation of the word when intended in a plural form.

Passage No. 1:

" ... the sky He constructed it , He raised its canopy and adjusted it , and darkened the night and brought out the forenoon, and the Earth after that He spread it, from its within He brought out its water and its pasture, and the mountains He firmly laid" [Surah 79: Verses 27–32].

Passage No. 2:

"...the one Who created the Earth in two days ..., and made mountains standing firm on its surface and bestowed His blessings on it and determined its sustenance in four days for those who seek, moreover He tended to the sky and it was smoke and commanded it and the Earth come you willingly or unwillingly and both said we do come in willing obedience,

So He adjusted the heavens as seven in two days and commanded every sky with its order and decorated the lowest sky with stars and with protection..." [Surah 41: Verses 9–12].

Passage No. 3:

"He is the one Who created for you all what is in the Earth, moreover tended to the sky and adjusted them as seven...."[Surah 2: Verse 29].

STAGES OF THE CREATION AND THE CONCOMITANCE OF STAGES

From carefully reviewing these passages, we can conclude that the Creation of the Heavens and Earth has been a dynamic ongoing process in which many events progressed concomitantly. For the sky, there was an initial construction, layout of dimensions, formation of the solar system, subsequent layering as seven heavens and decoration of the lowest sky. For the Earth, there was an initial birth, subsequent spreading of the surface, the appearance of water and pasture, the settling of mountains, and the estimation of sources of sustenance.

Because the Qur'an had repeatedly indicated that the Creation occurred in six stages, the sum of the described stages in passage No. 2 as eight should not be conflicting. This passage was mainly concerned with describing only creation and development of the Earth, as occurring in six stages, and describing the two stages of designing the heavens. If we are to count stages of creation of the Earth *independent* from stages of creation of the Heavens, we would clearly come up with numbers greater than eight, as passage No. 2 does not include the early stages of creation of the Heavens which were described in passage No. 1. The conclusion to be made here is that designation of the stages of the Creation as six actually means these stages include *concomitant* creation and development of *both* of the Heavens and the Earth.

The first two stages of the Creation were probably the longest in time and they included the gradual construction of the Heavens with galaxies and stars, the appearance of the solar system, along with the creation of the Earth in its preliminary form. The end of these two stages was likely when water and pasture appeared in the surface of Earth.

The subsequent four stages were relatively short and likely began with laying of the mountains and continued until all sources of sustenance appeared on the surface of the Earth, which were intended for the benefit of all future creatures. It also appears that, in stages three and four, while the Earth was being prepared for the emergence of intelligent life, the heavens continued their intended constructive process. Their final designing, layering into seven Heavens and decoration of the lowest Heaven took place, in stages five and six, concomitant with the last two stages of the Earth's development.

It should be noted that none of the three passages contain any reference to the existence of mankind on the surface of the Earth, a process which appears to take place later in time and is described, as an independent event, somewhere else in the Qur'an. Although passage No. 3 refers to all the preparations on the Earth which have been made "for you" it contains no reference to "created you."

THE CREATION BEGAN WITH THE HEAVENS

In passage 1, events of the Creation begins with construction of the heavens which mainly means galaxies and stars. This likely began shortly after the Big Bang explosion which is believed to have occurred approximately 12 billion years ago. Richard Morris related that approximately one billion years after the Big Bang, stars were "beginning" to light up the sky [2–30]. The sky was also raised, given dimensions and adjustment.

THE APPEARANCE OF NIGHT AND DAY

The reference to the appearance of the night and day is likely a reference to the birth and formation of the sun and the solar system including the Earth, which occurred approximately 4.6 billion years ago [3–127] and is required for preparation of the Earth for emergence of life .

THE SPREADING OF THE EARTH "AFTER THAT"

"After that" the Earth was spread at the surface after the night and day have become established. The spread of the Earth's surface is most likely a reference to the cooling of the surface and its conversion to a solid surface suitable for the emergence of life. Christian De Duve related that, because of frequent volcanic eruptions, falling comets and asteroids, the Earth was inhospitable to life for approximately half a billion years after its birth [4 –1]. Richard Morris related that, early in the Earth's history, impacts with asteroids and meteorites released so much heat that the surface of the Earth remained molten and the Earth did not have a solid surface till approximately 800 million years after its birth. By that time, the surface cooled, gradually turned solid and became suitable for the emergence of life [2– 44].

THE APPEARANCE OF WATER ON THE EARTH

Passage No. 1 proceeds to indicate that God, then, after spreading the Earth's surface, had brought out its water from" its within." Scientists think that early in the age of the Earth, earthquakes were frequent and led to creation of small fissures, from which molten lava began trickling upward for millions of years and volcanic activities released gas and water vapor. All this led to water condensation at the surface, and oceans began to form in the low lying areas [5– 268 & 269].

This process of generating the initial water to the surface of the Earth at its early development is entirely different from generation of rainfall, stream flow and groundwater as we would see in the chapter titled" Rainfall."

The Appearance of Pasture and Sustenance

With respect to development of pasture, a primitive form of sustenance, which is described in passage No. 1 to have also developed into the Earth following the appearance of water, scientists believe that the earliest form of life were in the form of blue-green algae, also known as cyanobacteria, which began the process of photosynthesis [5 – 269]. Debate continues whether life originated in the ocean, or originated on land and was subsequently swept into the ocean and for how long it remained confined to the ocean prior to appearing on land.

At any rate, James Schooley noted that when the capacity of photosynthesis came into the blue-green algae, the stage was set for the emergence of terrestrial life [6–3]. Photosynthesis produces carbohydrates which is the prime type of food from which other sources of food are manufactured by a living organism. Therefore, photosynthesis is the prime event initiating the pathway to production of pasture and other forms of sustenance for living organisms whether existed in the ocean or on land. "Photosynthesis is responsible for maintenance of all life on the planet, whether plants or animals," James Schooley related [6–89].

Photosynthesis and the generation of carbohydrates require the presence of sunlight, water and carbon dioxide as well as the pigment chlorophyll [7–271]. We had already learned from passage No. 1 that sunlight and water existed prior to the appearance of pasture. Carbon dioxide was abundant in the early Earth's atmosphere [5–269].

Chlorophyll A is the essential photosynthetic pigment in all plants, algae and cyanobacteria and had existed unaltered by evolution for about 3 billion years [7–274].

It is still unclear when photosynthesis first began. Christian De Duve related that some forms of life existed on Earth at least 3.5 billion years ago as fossilized imprints of bacteria "cyanobacteria" were found in rocks of that age, which are like the most advanced photosynthetic organisms present in the world today [4–1]. James Mauseth related that photosynthesis which is present in all green plants first arose about 2.8 billion years ago [7–9].

THE APPEARANCE OF MOUNTAINS

Meissner related that by the time the lithosphere (the Earth's crust) developed, ...large mountain chains began to form. About 1.9 billion years ago, the Skelefte mountain range developed in northern Europe. Between 1.2 to 0.9 billion years ago, a very long mountain belt stretching from the Greenvillan area in eastern North America to the Svecofennian region in southern Sweden developed [8–78].

It should be noted that the timing of mountain formation proceeds in the appropriate chronological order as outlined in passage No. 1. Assuming that the birth of the Earth occurred 4.6 billion years, spreading of its surface occurred between 500 million and 800 million years of the Earth's age, water appeared at approximately 800 million years of the Earth's age or 3.8 billion years ago, and the prime event which led the pathway to the development of pasture and sustenance was initiated anywhere between 3.5 billion years ago and 2.8 billion years ago. The appearance of mountain belts is believed to have begun approximately 1.9 billion years ago.

THE STATE OF "SMOKE"

The reference to God tending to the sky, while it was "smoke", is a reference to the state of gas clouds present in the universe from which galaxies and stars emerge. We had previously discussed the state of gas and "smoke" in the preceding chapter. The timing of this statement in passage No. 2 chronologically coincides with the development of sources of sustenance in the Earth. Did gas clouds exist at that time, or they have already been consumed by the formation of stars and galaxies which began shortly after the Big Bang? Fritzsch relates that stars continued to form since the beginning of the Creation, and some stars are presently twice the age of our sun while others are extremely young, younger than mankind [9–37]. He describes these gas clouds as "enormous" comprising "a great portion of the matter in the universe" and "are simply gigantic star factories" [9–39]. This leads to the conclusion that, at that time when God "tended to the sky," there were indeed large gas clouds or "smoke."

THE CONJUNCTIVE WORK BETWEEN THE SKY AND THE EARTH

While God was arranging sources of sustenance on the Earth, He commanded the Earth and the heaven to "come you" likely meaning to work together. This assignment was to proceed, by the order He directed to them, "willingly or unwillingly." This statement might likely indicate that, while sources of food are becoming available on the surface of the Earth, a conjunctive relationship between the Earth and the sky was required for preservation and advancement of these sources and for further propagation of life on Earth. We can only speculate on the possible meaning of this conjunctive relationship ....? ozone layer? water cycle ..etc.

THE ORDINANCE OF SEVEN HEAVENS

Then God fashioned the Heavens as seven and communicated to each heaven its specific order and decorated the lowest Heaven with lamps, meaning stars, and provided it with protection. We do not have any information in the Qur'an as to the nature of the seven Heavens, except that they have been fashioned in layers "the one Who created seven layered heavens" [Surah 67: Verse 3]. Therefore, no further discussion of this subject can be warranted. We only know that the lowest Heaven, because it is the one decorated with stars, is our own universe, and our scientific knowledge is confined only to this lowest Heaven.

It should not be concluded from the word "decorated" that stars have been all "created " at that time, for, the passage does not imply "initial creation" of the stars but rather, specifies that a "decorative" process or "shaping" of some type took place. It is presumed that large numbers of galaxies and stars have already been created when God began construction of the sky as described at the onset of passage No. 1, and that the formation of stars and galaxies has been a continuous process since shortly after the Big Bang.

REFERENCES

1. Bucaille, Maurice. *The Qur'an The Bible and Science.* Seghers. Paris, 1987.

2. Morris, Richard. *The Universe, the Eleventh Dimension, and Everything: What we know and how we knew it.* Four Walls Eight Windows. New York, 1999.

3. Fritzsch, Harald. *The Creation of Matter: The Universe from Beginning to End.* Basic Books. New York, 1984.

4. De Duve, Christian. The Beginnings of Life on Earth. *American Scientist*, Vol. 83, Sept-Oct 1995.

5. Parker, Barry. *Creation: The Story of the Origin and Evolution of the Universe*. Plenum Press. New York, 1988.

6. Schooley, James. *Introduction to Botany*. Thomson Delmar Learning. Albany, 1997.

7. Mauseth, James D. *Botany: An Introduction to Planet Biology*. Jones & Bartlett Publisher, Inc. Boston ,1998.

8. Meissner, Rolf. *The Little Book of Planet Earth*. New York Springer-Verlag, New York, 2002.

9. Fritzsch, Harald. *The Creation of Matter: The Universe from Beginning to End*. Basic Books. New York,1984.

3

Ascension in The Sky

".. AND WHOSOEVER GOD desires to guide, He will open his chest to Islam, and whosoever He desires to leave straying, He will make his chest tight and heavy as if he is ascending in the sky" [Surah 6: Verse 125].

This Qur'anic verse, which was revealed around the year 622 A.D. [1–87], describes the respiratory discomfort experienced by man when rising in the sky, which is now known to be the result of gradual decline in oxygen density with ascension in the sky. Some commentators attempted to equal ascension in the sky with mountain climbing, a modern scientific view which might have not been known in ancient and medieval times. Although some symptoms of discomfort attributed to mountain climbing, such as fever, headaches and vomiting, were described approximately two thousand years ago [2–295] and preceded the onset of the Qur'anic revelations, the *specific* question to be addressed is: Was this illness, during those times, attributed to the effect of *altitude* or was it attributed to something that had to do with the mountains themselves?

Dr. Charles Houston, who reviewed the literature on the history of "Men and Mountains" noted the absence of any reference to the altitude when reviewing experiences with mountain climbing during ancient and medieval times [3–8 to 11]. The earliest description of the effect of altitude was attributed to Jose d Acosta, a Spanish minister and explorer, in his account called "*The Natural and Moral History of the Indies*" in 1590 [3–12]. Acosta, when climbing the Indies mountains, described, in his own words, the air as " subtile and delicate as it is not proportionable with the breathing of man which requires a more gross and temperate air and I believe it is the cause that does so much alter the stomach and trouble all the disposition" [3-14]. Dr. Houston noted that, in the Andes, altitude sickness was familiar and in Bolivia and Chile was called "Antimony," and the symptoms were blamed on emanations from that ore. In other areas, rhubarb plants, primroses, heather, or mosses were alleged to produce pestilential vapors that made men sick [3-14]. In instances where volcanoes erupted in a mountain, the symptoms have been attributed to the volcanic fumes [3-14].

Considering, then, the fact that mountain climbing was not found to reflect the concept of altitude and elevation in the sky in those days, and considering that this Qur'anic verse specifically describes "ascension in the sky" and not mountain climbing, it is prudent to discuss this verse "just as" revealed and by its "literal" meaning.

Dr. Charles Houston described in "Exploration of the Heavens" that the first airborne man was Pilatre de Rozier who was flown in a balloon in 1783 up to a height of 3,000 feet for a trip which extended over several miles and lasted for approximately half an hour [3-51). Several years later, John Jeffries collected samples of air from different altitudes during his flight balloon in order to study the composition of these samples. Dr. Houston noted as balloonists "went higher into the thin cold air, the effects of altitude became more and more serious." Joseph Louis Gay-Lussac was described as having ascended ,in a balloon, to a height of 22,000 feet ,where he noted that "respiration was noticeably hampered "and his "pulse and respiratory rate were much accelerated" [3-55].

The Qur'an does not specifically mention oxygen, but it is now common knowledge that the respiratory distress which appears in the altitude is the result of a decrease in the amount of oxygen per unit of volume, scientifically known as the density of oxygen. Prior to the discovery of oxygen, came the discovery of existence of the Earth's atmosphere and the atmospheric pressure, made by Torricelli and Pascal in the later part of the 17th century ,which meant that air exhibited pressure on the surface of the earth [4–18 & 21]. This was followed by observations of Perier and Robert Boyle that the air "did get thinner and pressed less heavily on the earth the higher one went " [3–47] which meant there was a gradual decrease in the atmospheric pressure and decline of the air density with gradual ascension in the sky [5–32]. The discovery of oxygen as a component of the air took place in 1774 by two independent scientists [6–38]. Then Paul Bert, known as the father of altitude physiology, showed that breathing air under reduced pressure, as at altitude, was dangerous because of the decline in oxygen density with the decline in the air density. He demonstrated, using a chamber with reduced pressure inside to a level equivalent to 24,000 feet high, that significant symptoms occurred such as "dimming of vision and dulling of mind and difficulty with calculation." These symptoms were all promptly relieved by a few inhalations of oxygen [3–57].

To summarize,

– A Qur'anic verse was revealed in the year 622 A.D. describing heaviness and tightness of the chest when man ascend in the sky.

– Jose d Acosta, in 1590 ,during climbing of the Indies mountains, described the air as "subtile and delicate as it is not proportionable with the breathing of man."

– Pilatre de Rozier was considered to be the first airborne man, flown into a balloon in 1783, and shortly after that, Joseph Louis Gay-Lussac described respiratory difficulties when ascending,in a balloon, to 22,000 feet high.

— The existence of the Earth's atmosphere and that air exhibited pressure on the surface of the earth was discovered by Torricelli and Pascal in the later part of the 17th century.

— Shortly after that, Perier and Robert Boyle observed that the air "did get thinner and pressed less heavily on the earth the higher one went" which meant there was a gradual decline of the air density with gradual elevation in the sky.

— In 1774, the oxygen was discovered as a component of the air by two independent scientists.

— Then Paul Bert, known as the father of altitude physiology, showed that breathing air under reduced pressure, as at altitude, was dangerous because of the decline in oxygen density with the decline in the air density. He was able to relieve such symptoms by a few inhalations of oxygen.

The discovery was then complete.

REFERENCES

1. Abu Ala Maududi. *The Meaning of the Qur'an*, vol. 3. Islamic publications Ltd.. Lahore, 1988.

2. Marriott, Bernadette M. *Nutritional needs in cold and in high altitude environments*, [by Allen Cymerman]. National academy press, 1996.

3. Houston, Charles S. *Going Higher: the story of man and altitude.* Little Brown & Co.Boston,1987.

4. Cooke, Josiah Parsons. *Religion and Chemistry.* University of Virginia library, 1997.

5. Windelspecht, Michael. *Groundbreaking scientific experiments, inventions and discoveries of the 17th-century.* Praeger, Westport, Conn, 2002

6. Funk and Wagnalls *New Encyclopedia.* Vol. 20.

4

The Lowest Earth

"THE ROMANS WERE defeated, at the lowest earth but after their defeat they shall prevail. In a few years, for, to God belongs the order before and after, and then the believers shall rejoice" [Surah 30: Verse 2–4].

This Qur'anic verse, which was revealed around the year 615 [1–1049], refers to the defeat of the Eastern Romans (known as Byzantines) at the hands of the Persians who, as described by Haidon, "occupied Damascus and in 614 Jerusalem itself was taken, a particularly heavy blow to Byzantine morale " [2–43]. This event was also significant to Muslims because Palestine and Jerusalem were sacred to them, being the place they directed their prayers to in those early days of Islam [3, Vol 20–95]. While the Muslims morally supported the Christian Romans for being people of a faith, their enemy, the pagans of Mecca, were inspired by the victory of the pagan Persians and envisioned a future similar defeat of the Muslims at their own hands [4, Vol. 9–183].

The prophecy that, within several years, the Romans shall prevail, was first fulfilled in 622 when, led by Emperor Heraclius, they defeated the Persians in Issus [3, Vol. 14–311]. Subsequently, according to Haidon, "in a series of campaigns, beginning 622 and lasting until 628, Heraclius was able to outmaneuver the Persian forces in Astoria and Armenia and take the war to the heart of the Sassanid (Persian) empire" [2–45]. Palestine was subsequently recovered, and "in 630 the True Cross was returned in triumph to Jerusalem" [3, Vol. 13–69].

This review is not intended to emphasize the prophecy aspect of this verse because this is beyond the scope of this book. It was only presented to permit the reader to understand the text of this Qur'anic verse. This review is mainly concerned with the statement that the defeat had occurred "at the lowest earth" (*Adna Al Ardh*).

The Arabic-English Dictionary describes the word (*Adna*) as having two meanings, one is "closer" and the other is "lower" [5 –26]. It should be noted that in the text of this Qur'anic verse, the word was used as superlative adjective meaning the "closest" or the "lowest" earth (*Adna Al Ardh*). Most Qur'anic commentators, unaware of the impressive depression of the land in Palestine in the vicinity of the Dead Sea, where the noted defeat took place, interpreted the word (*Adna*) as "closest". Two Qur'anic commentaries, written in the 10th century and the 15th century respectively, interpreted this statement as the Romans were close to the Persians at the site of the battle [6, vol. 21–11 & 7–404]. Another Qur'anic commentary, published in 1934, described the "nearby" land as referring to Syria and Palestine" [1–1052]. A more recent Qur'anic commentary, published in 1981, explained the site of defeat as being in "territories adjacent to Arabia " [4, vol 9–181]. The confusion over interpretation implies that this phrase can not be clearly understood when interpreted to mean "closeness." If the verse was meant to describe "closeness," it would have defined to *whom* this earth was *closest*. To assume that the area of the battle was the closest to Muslim territories at that time, where this Qur'anic verse was revealed, would be geographically implausible, for the Muslim territory then consisted only of a portion of the city of Mecca with vast land that separates it from Palestine. Other territories such as Yemen, Egypt, and Abyssenia were significantly closer to the city of Mecca than Palestine [8–54 & Figure 1].

The Lowest Earth 37

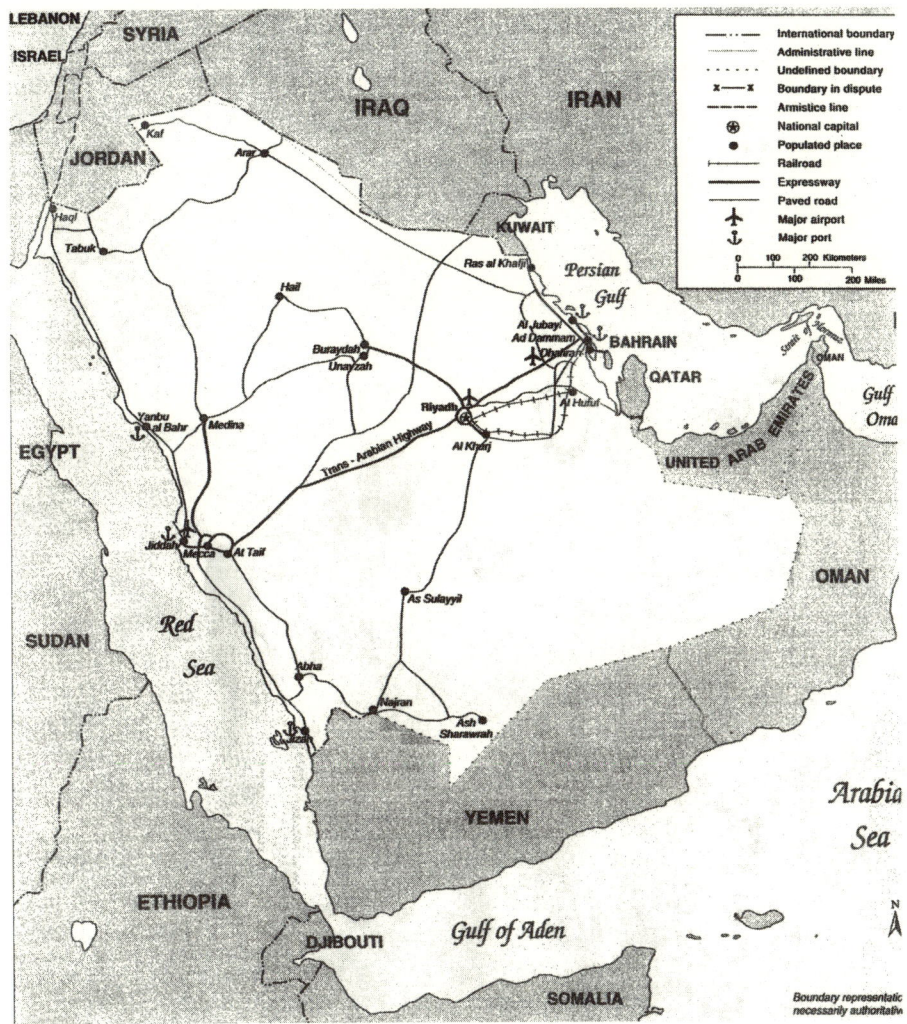

Figure 1: Location of the City of Mecca

[Picture Credit: *Saudi Arabia, a Country Study.*
Federal Research Division, United States government, 1993.]

Description of "the site of defeat" as being "the lowest earth" actually *defines* the area to where the Byzantines established their presence and where the Persians prevailed over them. Kreiger related that the Byzantine period "saw the last extensive settlement at the Dead Sea, till this century" [9–116]. She described the magnificent monastery built in the fifth century at Mar Saba which was "plundered by the Persians in the seventh century" [9–15], along with many other monasteries built in the Judean Desert, west of the Dead Sea, which were "decimated by the Persians when conquered Palestine at the beginning of the seventh century" [9 –80].

The Dead Sea is a part of the Rift Valley which, in the holy land, begins with the Jordan River in the north and extends south to the Dead Sea and beyond. The Jordan River originates at the anti Lebanon Mountains and extends south to the Sea of Galilee (Lake Tiberias), which lies 213 meters below sea level, and then to the Dead Sea [10–87 & Figure 2]. The Valley descends to a depth of 2600 feet below sea level at the bottom of the Dead sea. The Dead Sea itself lies 1296 feet below the Mediterranean and is the lowest point on earth [11–10]. Jericho, located at proximity to the Dead Sea is the lowest city on earth declining to 820 feet below sea level [11–237] and Jerusalem, sitting on elevation, is approximately 20 miles to the west [9 –122] separated from the Dead Sea by the Judean Desert.

Has it been known at that time (the seventh century) that this area was the lowest earth?

The first observation of the significant depression of the Dead Sea below the ocean, according to Kreiger, was reported in 1837, when Moore and Beke, noted that the level of the Dead Sea " appeared to be considerably lower than the ocean" using a method for determining height by observing the relative boiling point of water which

Figure 2: The Dead Sea area

[Picture Credit: *Israel, a Country Study.* Federal Research Division, United States government, 1990.]

would change with a change in the atmospheric pressure as a result of change in the height." However their estimate was only 500 feet below ocean level [9–42]. Two years later, Joseph Russegger gave a more accurate measurement using a barometric method, estimating the depth at −1400 feet [9–44] and around the same time, de Bertou arrived at an estimate of −1330 feet in 1841. A thorough investigation of the Dead Sea in the 19th century was conducted by William Lynch who, in 1848, led "the United States expedition to the River Jordan and the Dead Sea" [12–301]. Finally, in 1967, Neev and Emery, published their comprehensive studies using sophisticated tools, and measured the level, in 1963, as 398 m below sea level [13–37].

For the purpose of comparison, Perrin noted that the Dead Sea is four times as far below sea level as its American rival, Death Valley [9–xi]. With respect to the Death Valley in California, Joel Brooks was the first to guess, in 1861, that the floor of the Valley might actually be below sea level. In 1907 Biggs reported his survey which revealed a depth of slightly less than 287 feet and more recently, Lingenfelter reported a survey of the lowest point of the Valley to be 282 feet below sea level [14–3 & 4].

References

1. Ali A Yusuf. *The Meaning of The Holy Qur'an*, Amana Corp, 1983.
2. Haidon, John. *Byzantium in the Seventh Century: The Transformation of a Culture.* New York Cambridge University press, 1990.
3. Funk and Wagnals *New Encyclopedia.*
4. Abu Ala Maududi. *The Meaning of The Qur'an.* Islamic Publications [Pvt] Ltd.. Lahore, 1981.

5. Baalbaki, R .Al Mawred Al Quareeb. *Arabic- English Dictionary.* Dar El Elm Lilmalayin, 2001.

6. *Al Tabari Commentary of The Qur'an.* Dar Al Marefa, Beirut, Lebanon.

7. *Al Jalalan Commentary of The Qur'an.* Dar Ibn Katheer, Beirut, Lebanon.

8. Chapin Metz, Helen, editor. *Saudi Arabia –a country study.* The United States Government, 1993.

9. Kreiger, *Barbara: The Dead Sea: Myth, History ,and Politics.* NH University press of New England .Hanover, 1997.

10. Chapin Metz, Helen, editor. *Israel - a country study.* the United States Government, 1990.

11. Turner, George A. *Historical Geography of the Holy Land.* Baker Book House, 1973.

12. Lynch William F. *Narrative of the United States Expedition to the River Jordan and the Dead Sea.* Arno press, New York,1977 [original publication 1849].

13. Neev, David & Emery K.O. *The Dead Sea Depositional Processes and Environments of Evaporites.* The Sate of Israel. Ministry of Development, Geological Survey Bulletin No. 41. Jerusalem, 1967.

14. Lingenfelter, Richard. *Death Valley the Amargosa: a Land of Illusion.* Berkeley University of California press,1986.

5

The Descended Iron

"AND WE SENT down iron, in which there is strength and benefits to mankind " [Surah 57: Verse 25].

This Qur'anic verse describes the fall of iron to the Earth for the intended purpose of providing benefits to mankind. This process is presently known as meteorites. *The American Heritage Dictionary of the English Language* defines the word meteorite as "a stony or metallic mass of matter that has fallen to the earth's surface from outer space" [1].

THE FALL OF IRON

Iron falls to the surface of the Earth, contained within meteorites which are divided into three major groups. The first is iron meteorites composed mainly of iron and contain some other metals such as nickel and precious metals [2–26]. All the world's great meteorites are iron according to Norton [3–245]. The second class is the stony meteorites which are the most common type and are composed mainly of rocks which resemble the earth crust but, unlike the earth crust, they also contain iron metals alloyed with nickel, similar in composition to iron meteorites [3–176]. The third class is stony- irons which contain about 50 percent each of metal and rocks and are extremely rare [3–235]. Rubin defined the origin of meteorites as arising from the moon, from Mars or from asteroids [4–26].

Lewis noted that the fall of iron from the sky has been known in ancient cultures, such as the Chinese, Greek and Egyptian. However, ancient and medieval accounts of the fall of meteorites had confused fact and fancy. He related the account of Pliny the elder in the first century A.D. describing the fall of iron, in which he spoke about "blood and fire" falling from the skies followed by the falls of "milk, blood and flesh." In his description of another iron fall, Pliny spoke of a rain of "wool" and "clanging armor and sounding trumpets in the sky" which accompanied the event [2–14]. In Greek classical culture through the Middle Ages, the description bore even more fantasies with descent attributed to the fall of offspring from the affairs of immortal gods with mortals [2–16].

Lewis emphasized that European culture, prior to the advent of the 19th century, had rejected the concept of anything falling from the sky [2–11]. This rejection, according to Norton, was largely dictated by the church doctrine as well as by the prevalence of Aristotle's teaching that stones could not fall from heaven since this would violate the doctrine of heavenly perfection [3–36]. Even when fall of objects from the sky was entertained, it was considered to accompany violent thunderstorms and was attributed to "earthly" particles which accumulate inside clouds and fall back to the ground due to their heavy weight [3–36]. "The first meteorites expert in the world was the German scientist Ernest F.F. Chladni (1756–1827) who diligently searched for reports of meteorite falls in the old records," and accepted that these objects had indeed fallen from the sky [2–24]. Transformation of the opinion in France took longer, until 1803, when a shower of 25 hundred stones fell in L'Agile, Normandy. Around that time, three famous French scientists, Biot, Laplace and Poisson, joined in accepting the legitimacy of this fall [2–25].

In the United States, an equivalent of the Normandy meteorite fell in Connecticut in 1807 and was studied by Silliman and Kingsley, professors at Yale, who pronounced it as credible. A highly prominent politician and scientist rejected the claim finding it difficult to believe "that stones should fall from the sky." This, however changed in 1819 when the American physician William G. Reynolds described his four theories for explanation of the phenomena and the concept of the fall of extraterrestrial material has, since, become acceptable [2–26].

BENEFITS TO MANKIND

This Qur'anic verse indicates that iron is descended to Earth so it may be used for its strength, which refers to various weaponry and equipment made from steel and iron normally extracted from iron ores [5–34810]. The verse also relates that iron has other benefits to mankind. Other benefits derived from iron are nutrition related and include the presence of iron in the earth crust which is normally absorbed by plants and subsequently passed on to animals and humans [6]. Some other benefits of the fall of iron could also include, as we would see below, replenishing other valuable precious metals present in meteorites, normally alloyed with iron and known as siderophile or iron loving, back into the earth crust.

Iron meteorites are the largest known meteorites, many times larger and more massive than any stony meteorite, and are very durable and resistant to fracturing and weathering [3–215]. These characteristics actually allow them to penetrate the Earth's atmosphere and remain relatively intact by the time they reach the ground [7–80]. They contain large amounts of iron-nickel metal alloys which are very rare in the earth crust with the iron being by far the dominant component [3–177] and represent almost the only source of native iron on the surface of the earth [8–102]. The fall of such meteorites may replenish iron back into the earth's surface in the form of metal ores.

Scientists believe that the Earth originally had its iron uniformity distributed throughout, which meant there was considerable iron near the surface. The Earth's iron has gradually sunk to the core due to its heavy weight where is now located [7–34]. Other precious metals with heavy weight such as platinum, gold and their relatives, alloyed with iron, had also sunk with the iron to the Earth's core [9–19]. The American scientist Luie Alvarez noted that these precious metals were ten thousand times more common in meteorites than in the earth crust. He had shown that these metals in the Earth's sedimentary rocks and clay had in fact come from meteorites [9–19].

Stony meteorites are the most common type of meteorites and generally resemble the earth crust rocks except, unlike the earth rocks, they contain smaller amounts of iron nickel alloys [3–176] with iron being the predominant component of these alloys. Due to their abundance on the surface of the Earth, stony meteorites likely renew iron which is incorporated within the earth crust.

Smaller meteorites are usually slowed down by the Earth's atmosphere and land rather gently on the surface of the Earth [10–19]. Larger masses, however, travel relatively unaffected by the atmosphere causing an impact on the ground known as craters. Studies of the craters distributed throughout the Earth's surface have relatively recently been conducted. The Australian astronomer Duncan Steel estimated that over the past three billion years or so, at least two million such craters were formed on the continent, the majority of craters counted were created by iron meteorites [7–160]. It is then quite likely that iron falling from space had contributed to continuous supply of the Earth with iron during its maturity. Norton showed a schematic description of the events when such large meteorite strike the earth. The resulting shock wave leads to creation of crater and fragmentation of the meteorite along with the rocks at the site of the collision with subsequent fall back occurring in the crater site and the surrounding earth [3–125]. Shoemaker after extensive geological examination of what is known as the Meteor Crater in Arizona, which is estimated to have fallen approximately fifty thousand years ago, documented the presence of fragments of the original iron mass scattered over hundreds of square miles around the site of impact [10–21].

Conclusion

1. This Qur'anic verse, revealed approximately 1400 years ago, indicates that iron does fall from the sky with the intended purpose of providing benefits to mankind. This statement was clear and unaccompanied by fables or fantasies or description of living objects falling from the sky as seen in other ancient accounts.

2. This Qur'anic statement was a contrary to future notions in medieval times and modern Europe that nothing can possibly fall from the sky; such notions remained prevalent till the onset of the 19th century.

3. Scientific evidence has shown that iron falling from the sky does provide benefits to mankind as this Qur'anic statement indicated. These benefits may include replenishing iron ores, renewing iron into the earth crust which has nutritional benefits to living creatures, and providing precious metals, which are normally alloyed with iron, back into the earth crust.

References

1. *The American Heritage Dictionary of the English Language,* Fourth Edition. Houghton Mifflin Company, 2003.

2. Lewis, John S. *Rain of Iron and Ice: The Very Real Threat of Comet and Asteroid Bombardment.* Addison Wesley, Reading MA,1997.

3. Norton, O Richard *Rocks from Space. Mountain* Press Publishing Company, 1994.

4. Rubin, Alan E. *American Scientist.* Volume :85 . Issue :1.January – February 1997. The Scientific Research Society, 1997.

5. *The Columbia Encyclopedia*, Sixth Edition. Columbia University Press, New York, 2000.

6. *The Columbia Electronic Encyclopedia*, Sixth Edition. Columbia University Press, 2003.

7. Barnes-Svarney, Patricia. *Earth Destroyer or New Frontier?.* Plenum Press. New York,1996.

8. Pough, Frederick H., Scovil, Jeffrey. *A Field Guide to Rocks and Minerals.* Houghton- Mifflin Trade and Reference. Boston, 1996.

9. Dauber, Phillip M., Muller Richard A. *The Three Big Bangs: Comet Crashes, Exploding Stars, and the Creation of the Universe.* Perseus Books. Cambridge, MA., 1996.

10. Morrison, David. *Cosmic Catastrophes.* Plenum Press. New York, 1989.

6

Mountains are Pegs

"... AND WE MADE the mountains as pegs." [Surah 78: Verse 7].

In this Qur'anic verse, which was revealed in the early seventh century [1–1672], the mountains are described as pegs, which means having roots inside the earth so they resemble pegs.

In the 19th century, the American geologist James Hall in 1859 made the first observation that rocks of the same age are many times thicker under the Appalachian Mountains than under the low land. Subsequently, other geologists found this to be true with other mountain belts including the Himalayas, the Alps and the Andes. A depth of five and eight miles of strata was found underneath such mountain belts compared to a few thousand feet under the adjacent continental plates [2–506 & Figure 1]. Under the Sierra Nevada, the strata extended down to approximately 60 kilometers [2–524] and under the Himalayas down to 85 kilometers. Because this thickness was thought to be caused by downward folding of the earth crust, the American geologist James Dana in the year 1873 called it "geosyncline" which means "great earth downfold" [3–103].

When the plate tectonics theory emerged in the 1960's, the theory of mountain formation was revised. Some mountains are now believed to be volcanic in origin, and some are caused by vertical movements along faults such as in the Sierra Nevada mountains. The great mountains of the Earth are believed now to have originated as a result of compressional forces which resulted from convergence of continental or oceanic plates [3–439)].

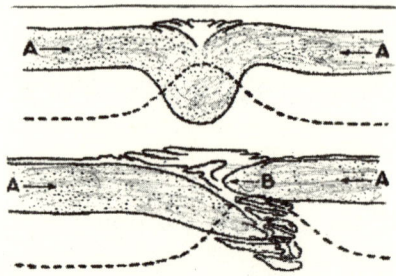

Figure 1: Symmetrical and asymmetrical types of mountain roots.

[Picture Credit: Umbgrove JHF, *The Pulse of the Earth*. Martinus Nijhoff Publishers, the Hague, 1947.]

When a collision of an oceanic and a continental plate takes place, the oceanic plate, having greater density and significantly less thickness, descends underneath the overriding continental plate, a process called subduction, and the area in which this process occurs is called subduction zone. The descending plate can reach a depth of approximately one hundred kilometers into the interior of the earth and begin to melt due to high temperature producing molten rocks and magma which invade the overriding plate and produce changes in the overriding plate ultimately leading to formation of mountains and their roots [3–441]. The Andes Mountains of South America were produced in this manner [4–26].

When two continental plates, which are normally much thicker than oceanic plates, converge, subduction does not occur due to comparable thickness of the continental plates. They simply push against each other and one continent rides onto the other near the convergence margins creating a double thickness of the crust ,near these margins, leading to formation of mountains [4–443]. The Himalayas were produced, approximately 50 million years ago, by the convergence of two continental plates [4–27].

Regardless how mountain chains form, the existence of mountain roots; a substantial thickness of the strata underneath mountain belts, was first described in the 19th century. Elaboration on the origin and manner of formation were described by geologists of the 20th century.

REFERENCES

1. Ali A Yusuf. *The Meaning of The Holy Qur'an*. Amana Corp, 1983.

2. Gilluly, James. *Principle of Geology*. W.H Freeman. San Francisco, 1958.

3. Woodhead, James A. *Geology – Magill's Choice*. Pasadena, Calif. Salem Press, 1999.

4- Silverstein, Alvin; Silverstein, Virginia B.; Nunn, Laura Silverstein. *Plate Tectonics – Science Concepts*. Brookefield, Conn. Twenty-First Century Books, 1998.

7

Human Reproduction

VERSE NO. 1: "We created man of a complex multi elemental tiny amount of semen" [Surah 76: Verse 2].

Verse No. 2: "God created man from a leech like thing" [Surah 96: Verse 2].

Verse No. 3: "Then We created the semen into a leech like thing then We created this into a morsel of meat then We created the morsel into bones then We clothed bones with muscles and then We had developed it into another shape" [Surah 23: Verse 14].

Verse No. 4: "...from a tiny amount of semen then from a clinging thing then from a morsel of meat which is formed and unformed" [Surah 22: Verse 5].

Examining the Qur'anic view on reproduction from conception to birth, reveals repeated emphasis on *transformation* of the product of conception. That is, development occurs in *stages*. This might appear as common knowledge at this time, but it was not until 1827 when von Baer first described the principal stages in the development of the mammalian embryo [1--370]. Prior to that, the prevalent hypothesis was the concept of "preformation." This means that a *complete* animal, in a miniature form, was believed to exist in the germ and would only need to enlarge by *growth* of its parts [1–364]. The germ was believed to be either the female egg or the male sperm. Scientists who believed that the offspring was present fully formed in the female egg included Swammerdam, Malpighi and others. Scientists who believed that a preformed individual was present in the male sperm were called the spermists. They included Leeuwenhoek who first discovered the male sperm under a primitive microscope and Nicolas Hartsoeker who first published pictures, in 1694, of preformed men which he had claimed to have seen inside the sperm with the aid of a microscope [1–364]. The pictures showed the sperm encasing a tiny human figure called the homunculus [Figure 1].

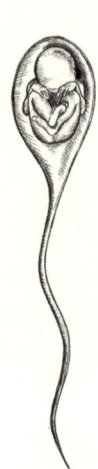

Figure 1:
A drawing which resembles the tiny human figure, within the sperm, called the homunculus by the spermists in the 17th century.

1. THE SEMEN IS A HIGHLY COMPLEX LIQUID

Verse No. 1 reads "We created man of a complex tiny amount of semen." The Arabic word for tiny amount is "*nutfa*." This word, literally translated, means tiny amount, but as it is used in the process of human reproduction, it indicates a tiny amount of semen. In fact, in another verse, the word "*nutfa*" is defined as being related to the semen" was he (man) not made of a tiny amount "*nutfa*" from the semen which is normally ejaculated?" [Surah 75: Verse 37].

Sigman and Howards described the complexity of the semen as being composed of multiple elements:

– The sperm which number in millions, normally 70 to 80 million per milliliter, and originate in the testes [2–1295].

– The fluid secreted from the seminal vesicles, which are located above the prostate gland. This fluid contains a substance which gives the semen a gel consistency needed for the proper placement of the semen in the female uterus [3–89].

– The prostatic fluid which is responsible for liquefying the semen approximately 20 to 30 minutes after entering the vagina, a process which allows the sperm to spread higher into the uterus [3–89].

– The secretion from Cowper's glands which are located below the prostate [2–1291].

2. **THE FIRST STAGE** in human reproduction, which involves the union between the female egg and the male sperm is known scientifically as fertilization. **The second stage** which occurs after the fertilized egg enlarge by multiplication of the inner cells is known as implantation, a process by which the fertilized egg, now known as the "blastocyte" attaches itself to the lining of the uterus and this, according to Craven and Wads, occurs on days five or six of the development [4 – 30]. This process of attachment is described in the Qur'an in the Arabic word (*Alaqa*) which had two defined meanings. The first is "something which cling," as in Verse No. 4, which reads "... from a tiny amount of semen then from something which cling" [Surah 22: Verse 5]. The word "then from" indicates a second stage to take place. Compare this scientifically documented process of "attachment" to the Qur'anic word "cling."

A second precise meaning of the word (*Alaqa*) in Arabic is "leech." In fact, this is the accepted translation of the word in Arabic medical terminology. *The Arabic English Dictionary* lists this specific meaning as the only translation of the word [5–283]. Verse No. 2 reads: "God created man from a leech like thing (*Alaq*)" [Surah 96: Verse 2], with the word (*Alaq*) being the reference word for the class leech in Arabic. There is substantial resemblance between the blastocyte attachment to the lining of the uterus with subsequent invasion of its blood vessels and the leech attachment to its host and invading its blood vessels. Craven and wards described how the blastocyte begins to invade the maternal circulation during the second week of pregnancy as: some outer cells of the blastocyte termed x cells migrate away from its shell and erode into maternal blood vessels that maternal blood may be seen in the shell surrounding the blastocyte during that time. This process is accompanied by dilation of the maternal blood vessels [4–30].

Buchsbaums and Pearses noted that the leech is remarkable for possessing "clinging suckers." In sucking blood, the leech attaches to an animal or a human by the posterior sucker and applies the anterior sucker to the skin making a painless wound with the aid of small jaws inside the mouth [6–314]. This process continues till the digestive tract of the leech is filled with blood. During this process, the leech produces a substance which causes dilation of the host blood vessels [6–316] in a manner which resembles dilation of the maternal blood vessels invaded by the blastocyte. Aside from invasion of the host blood vessels, the leech clings to its host painlessly that field workers may be unaware of leeches hanging from their ankles like bushes of grapes [3–316], a process which resembles the clinging of the blastocyte to the endometrial lining.

3. **THE THIRD STAGE** of development is called the "embryo," which is designated as such approximately two weeks following conception. Cunningham et al described the transition of the blastocyte into embryo which is now engulfed by the uterus wall and surrounded by a soft shell which develops villi [or processes], filled with maternal blood [7–94]. Craven and Wards estimate the size of the embryo at this stage as being at a minimum of 1.4 cm and its weight as being at a minimum of five grams [4–32].

In describing this stage, the Qur'an proceeds in Verse No. 4 to read "...then from a chewed morsel of meat which is formed and unformed." Again, the words "then from" indicates a new stage in development. This Qur'anic description of the embryo at this stage, as being a piece of chewed meat, appears in agreement with the scientific description of the embryo with respect to its size, weight and shape. The statement "formed" likely indicates that some systems have already been formed. The statement "unformed" likely indicates that :

– The embryo contained an unformed structures such as the amniotic cavity or the yolk sac.

– The embryo contained some structures which have been formed but others which have not as yet been formed.

– Or it could refer to the soft shell which surrounds the embryo and called "syncytium," which Cunningham et al repeatedly described as an "amorphous" structure [7–88], with "amorphous" meaning "unformed."

4. Beginning at week 5, the bony structures begin to appear in various areas of the embryo including the spine and the ribs, the head and neck and the limbs [8] leading to formation of the skeleton with the embryo assuming a new shape dominated by the shape of the skeleton. By the Qur'anic wording, the morsel is now transformed into a skeleton [Verse No. 3].

The limbs begin to form at the end of week 4 by the mesoderm layer, which is the middle layer of the embryo, pushing out the covering external layer and forming what's called "limb buds" [Figure 2]. The "clothing "of the bones, described above in Verse No. 3,

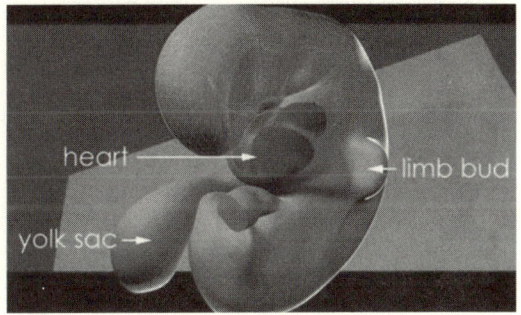

Figure 2: The limb buds
[Picture Credit: Collaborative Online Embryology The Visible Embryo Project. www.llnl.gov/atp/visem/visem2.ppt. United States government]

deserves special attention. Sweeney related that the bone and cartilage structures form inside the limbs, while cells which form the skeletal muscles are "outsider" that migrate from another region in the mesoderm [8–88] and must travel some distance to their target destination

[8–128]. Connective tissue structures develop in the limb and direct the organization of skeletal muscle masses from muscle cells precursors migrating from the other region [8–88]. This description appears compatible with the Qur'anic statement of "clothing" of the muscles over the bones.

Finally, the "fetus", which is called as such beginning as of the third month, will have complete organ formation by this time and will continue to grow by multiplication of the cells as well as enlargement in size and attainment of biological functions [8–6], a process which continues up to the time of delivery. Description of this fetal development could be what was meant by the Qur'anic statement in Verse No. 3, "We had developed it into *another* shape."

References

1. Mason, Stephen, F. *A History of the Sciences.* Collier Books. New York, 1962.
2. Sigman, Mark & Howard, Stuart, *S. Campbell's Urology*, 7th edition, WB Saunders company, 1998.
3. Creasy & Resnik. *Maternal Fetal Medicine* [Robert H. Glass], WB Saunders company, 1994.
4. Craven C & Ward K. Danforth's *Obstetrics and Gynecology*, 8th edition. Lippincot Williams & Wilkins, 1999.
5. Al Mawrid Al Quareeb. *A Pocket Arabic English Dictionary*, 11th edition. Dar el elm Lilmalayin. Beirut, Lebanon, 2001.
6. Buchsbaum R&M and Pearse J&V. *Animals Without Backbones*, third edition. The University of Chicago press. Chicago, 1987.
7. Cunningham et al. Williams *Obstetrics*, 21st edition. McGraw Hill, 2001.
8. Sweeney L. *Basic Concepts in Embryology.* McGraw Hill, 1998.

8

Water in the Living Organism

"WE CONSTRUCTED OF water every living thing" [Surah 21: Verse 30].

"and God created every moving creature from water" [Surah 24: Verse 45].

Water as the major component of every living organism, whether human or animal, was described in the Qur'an in these two verses. Relatively recent scientific studies addressed the composition of human and animal body and documented the major contribution of water to this composition.

In 1949, Soberman et al used a substance called Antipyrine to measure total body content of water in man. They selected this substance because it is rapidly distributed throughout body water. They concluded that water contributed to 60 to 65 percent of total body weight. They described two earlier studies which were conducted by Best et al in 1945 and Gamble et al in 1947 who made almost the same conclusion that the body consisted of 65 to 70 percent of water [1].

Earlier, in 1927, Skelton studied tissue content of water in the cats by obtaining samples from various organs. These samples were weighed and placed in an electric oven at temperatures ranging from 102 to 104 C till the sample weight became constant. The difference was calculated as the amount of evaporated water. He also described the work of other investigators who studied body water content in other animals. Bischoff in 1863, Engles in 1904 and Herman in 1891 studied the man. Donaldson in 1915 studied the rats and Engles in 1904 and Stewart in 1921 studied the dogs. Krause in 1884 studied the rabbits. They concluded that water was the major component of the body in all studied animals. The ratio of water to total body weight had varied slightly from 63 percent in man to 68.8 percent in rabbits. These investigators, independently, studied water content of various tissues in these animals such as skin, muscles, brain, spinal cord, liver, kidney, blood and spleen. They concluded that water content of the corresponding organs were almost the same in these animals [2].

The work of these investigators substantiates the statements made in these Qur'anic verses with respect to the composition of human and animal body. Some early Qur'anic commentators interpreted the word "created "in the first verse as implying "initiating" the creation of every moving thing from "semen" which had been compared to water. This appears to be unlikely due to the following reasons :

– In every instance the Qur'an referred to the semen as water, the description of water was specific such as "emitted water" [Surah 86: Verse 6], "despised water" [Surah 32: Verse 8] and the description was confined to man and did not extend to any other creature.

– Although the semen is the method of reproduction for humans and higher animals, it is not the reproductive means for lower animals or plants. Both verses refer to "every" living organisms or creature.

– The first verse relates that "God constructed of water every living thing" [Sureah 21: Verse 30]. The word "constructed" is a translation of the word "*jaalna*" in Arabic, which precisely means designing and constructing.

REFERENCES

1. Soberman et al. *The Use of Antipyrine in Measurement of Total Body Water in Man.* J Biol Chem 179 :31 – 42, May 1949.

2. Skelton, H. *The Storage of Water by Various Tissues of the Body.* Archives of Internal Medicine 14, 140,1927.

9

Qur'anic Comments on The Honeybee

AND YOUR LORD had *commanded* the honeybee that you shall make your homes in the hills, trees and men's habitations. *Then*, you shall *feed* on *all* the *fruits* then, you shall follow the *paths of your Lord* which were made *accessible* to you, there comes from *her abdomen* a liquid of diverse hue which contains healing for mankind. Verily, in this there is a sign for those who give thought [Surah 16: Verses 68 & 69].

The honeybee is a highly social insect which lives as colonies in trees, caves or human made beehives. Morse noted that the words colony, nest and hive are often used interchangeably [1–93]. The colony consists of a queen whose main function is laying eggs, male drones which are beneficial in mating with the queen to produce the fertilized eggs and female workers who perform all the tasks of the colony with the exception of laying eggs [1–484]. The workers forage away from the colony's nest to collect nectar from flowers and plants in order to manufacture honey which the colony use as a source of food and collect pollen which is used as a source of protein for the newly emerging bee [2–131]. They return back to their hive to unload the crop. Bees produce wax, from specific pockets located on the underside of the worker, to build the honeycomb in which honey is stored [2–209].

Due to its dedication, precision and social organization, the bee was sacred through the ages. In ancient times, it was considered to have descended from Paradise or sent down directly from gods [3–263]. It comes as prudent for the Qur'an to make specific comments on the honeybee for being one manifestation of God's great creations. Although these comments may sound as common knowledge at this time, but having been made in the early part of the 7th century, they deserve special attention from scientific and chronological standpoint.

Origin of The Bee

The Greek naturalist Aristotle, in the 4th century B.C., thought the bee young normally fetches from flowers such as the reed and olive because the better the olive harvest, the more numerous the swarms were [4–17]. Similarly, the Roman author Virgil, in the first century A.D., thought the "bees, unmated, gather their children in their mouths from leaves and fragrant herbs" [5–15]. Another notion which originated in Egypt and was promoted by Virgil and others including Columella, a spaniard who lived in first century Rome, was that the bee could spontaneously be generated from carcass of an ox or calf [6–11]. According to More, this notion "persisted almost into modern times" and the Dictionarium Rusticum in 1704 described generation of bees from a carcass [6–11 & 12].

This Qur'anic verse does not promote such beliefs which prevailed up to the onset of modern times. It specifies that the bee would first exist in her homes on trees or in mountain caves or human made beehives. *Then*, the bee would approach plants and begin to perform its intricate functions. Attempting to explain the logic behind the theory of "spontaneous generation of the bee", More believed that the insect produced from carcass was a drone- fly known as Eristalis tenax which resembled the look of the bee [6–12] while Gojmerac thought "the rib cage made a good home for a bee swarm" [7–10].

THE ORIGIN OF HONEY

With respect to the origin of honey, Virgil thought it was a "heavenly gift from the air" [5–14] while the Roman naturalist Pliny the elder, who also lived in the first century, thought it originates "either from the sweat of the sky or the saliva of the stars" [4–129]. The Roman philosopher Celsus who lived in the second century A.D. affirmed previous concepts by Aristotle and others that honey was made from dew, and wax was obtained by the bee from flowers [4–125]. Style concluded that "though there seemed to be a vague understanding that the quality of honey was related to the quality of the flowers in which it was stored, it was at least 1000 years before the crucial relationship between flowers and bees became clear" [5–15]. One thousand years after Virgil and Pliny is approximately 400 years after this Qur'anic verse was revealed.

This Qur'anic verse specifies that honeybee must feed on fruits, which are flowering plants, *first*, and as a *result* of that a new liquid would be produced by her, therefore establishing a "cause and effect" relationship between feeding on flowers and honey production long before this process was firmly established through scientific means. Linnaeus, the founder of the modern classification system for plants and animals who lived in the 18th century was the first to give honeybee its scientific name. He initially named the honeybee Apis mellifera, which means (honey bearing) and later in 1761 [6–36] changed it to Apis mellifica (honey maker) when he realized that she actually *made* the honey [5–31] which suggests that the knowledge of the honeybee as being a manufacture of honey was concluded around his time. English and French speakers, according to Style, tend to continue to use mellifera while in German and other languages mellifica is the preferred term [5–31].

THE FEMALE WORKER

The sex of the worker, as well as the ruler, had remained a mystery for many centuries. Development of the microscope and creation of the observation hive significantly contributed to modern knowledge of the bee, and in 1637 Richard Remnant, was able to visualize the worker genitals under glass and described them as female [6–113]. Swammerdam, in the 17th century, was able to clearly identify the sex of the ruler, through dissection, as being a queen rather than a king [6–113].

It is now known that all honeybee workers who collect the nectar, produce the honey and build the honeycomb are females [8–91]. The function of the male drones is only to mate and they are incapable of working in the hive or collecting nectar or pollen [9–30]. This conclusion is in agreement with this Qur'anic verse which specifically referred to the honeybee worker as "female" when describing various stages of her work performance.

FLOWERS OR PLANTS AND THEIR MULTITUDE

This Qur'anic verse indicates that God had commanded the bee to feed on fruits, which are flowering plants, in order to formulate honey. Free described how the bee collects nectar from flowers, which is stored into her abdomen, and is subsequently converted to honey by adding the enzyme "invertase" from its own glands [10–54]. The Qur'anic word "all" indicating "multitude" of flowering plants deserves special attention. Winston related that a honeybee worker may visit well over 1000 flowers to collect a nectar load and that workers seeking nectar may make up to 150 trips in a single day [8–172]. The British scientist, J Arthur Thomson estimated that honeybees from one hive will visit more than a quarter million blooms in a single day [11–58]. Robinson and Oertel referred to estimates of the total number of plants from which honeybees gather nectar or pollen or both in the United States and Canada as being as high as 3000 different species [2 – 286].

Nectar is normally secreted by specialized glands called nectaries located either in the flowers (floral) or on any above ground structures (extra floral) [7–164]. Extra floral nectarines, according to Morse, can be located on leaves, stems, bracts, petioles ,stipules or developing fruits and they produce nectar 24 hours a day while floral nectaries secrete nectar only during one relatively short period in the day [1–163]. This Qur'anic verse describes the honeybee as feeding on the "fruits, the flowering plants" rather than only on the "flowers," which could indicate that nectar gathering is not limited to the flower component of the flowering plant and possibly an indirect knowledge of the existence of extra floral locations.

EXTRACTION FROM THE ABDOMEN

Like other insects, honeybee is anatomically composed of three parts: head, thorax and abdomen. This Qur'anic verse describes the secretion of honey by the honeybee as occurring from her abdomen. The nectar and water are normally collected by the honeybee through her mouth parts and stored in the honey stomach which is an expendable bag that occupies much of the abdominal cavity when full. When the bee returns to the hive, it regurgitate the crop from her abdomen [8–32]. The process of converting nectar to honey actually begins while nectar is being collected in the honey stomach through glandular secretions and subsequently completed in the hive and stored in the honeycomb cells [6–36].

It should be clear that this mechanism of production is unique to honey. For, unlike honey, pollen which is consumed by the newly emerging bee is collected by an entirely different mechanism through adherence to the pollen basket located on the hind leg and transported to the hive for this purpose [9–50]. The bee milk or royal jelly which is manufactured by the honeybee in order to feed the brood in their larval stage is secreted from glands in the worker's head and not from her abdomen [9–49]. Wax which is used to build the honeycomb is secreted from wax pockets located on the underside of the workers [2–209]. More credited the French physicist Rene Antoine Reaumur of making in 1740, through his own glazed hive and microscope, the definite observation that the honeybee worker feed its young with regurgitated food [6–115].

Paths of the Lord

This Qur'anic verse then indicates that God had commanded the bee to follow the "paths of her Lord" which were made "accessible" to her. This statement was interpreted by some Qur'anic commentators to be a reference to the "dance phenomenon" which bees perform after returning to the hive from foraging trips in order to recruit other workers to a source of food. This phenomenon was discovered by von Frisk in the first half of the 20th century and came to be known as the dance language [12–56]. However the exact placement of this statement within the Qur'anic verse actually occurs *after* the worker had extracted the nectar from plants and *prior* to unloading it from her abdomen which normally occurs in the hive. Therefore, this statement appears to be descriptive of the navigation process the honeybee assumes in order to return back to its home hive which could be several thousand meters away.

This navigation process is essential for the forager considering its extremely poor vision which was estimated as 20/2000 and the fact that her "home tree is an indistinct blur until she is only a few meters away" [12–124]. The scientific work which led to understanding of this process is attributed mainly to von Frisk and subsequently to Lindauer and Gould and Gould in the 20th century [12–125].

Gould and Gould described four independent components of this navigational process, each could be instrumental when the others are absent:

1. The sun, which is the primary compass honeybees use for orientation. This was documented by the experiments conducted by von Frisk and his students. Gould and Gould, in discussing the experiments, concluded that "obviously, bees do not learn to recognize the sun by personal experience; instead, they are born with a crude but diagnostic rule" [12–128].

2. When the sun is behind the clouds or trees and under overcast, the bees orient themselves during flying by the polarized light which von Frisk had initially described. This phenomenon requires the honeybees to be able to see approximately 10 degrees of the sky in order to orient their flight [12–141].

3. The polarized light may not be useful when no part of a blue sky is visible such as under overcast. In such circumstances, honeybees use previously known landmarks such as a familiar lake, roads or forest edges [12–148].

4. When the above three navigational systems are unavailable, the honeybee can be guided by the earth's magnetic field. Gould and Gould discovered, along with two geologists, that honeybees can be quite magnetic. They discovered magnetic crystals which are present within specialized cells in the honeybee abdomen which would have magnetic orientation only in the presence of external magnetic fields such as the Earth's [12–154].

The navigation system of the honeybee appears to be composed of four *natural* phenomena, which would normally be the destination of the Lord and could qualify for description as "paths of the Lord "which the honeybee follows as commanded by Him. Gould and Gould commented that it is illogical to think that the honeybee had the capability of acquiring all these skills but they should be thought of as "pre wired."

REFERENCES

1. Morse, Roger A, Flottum, Kim. *The ABC & XYZ of Bee Cultures*, 40th Edition. The A.I. Root Co. Medina, Ohio, 1990.

2. Dadant & Sons. *The Hive and the Honey Bee*. Dadant & Sons. Hamilton, Illinois, 1982.

3. Johnson James W. The Neo-Classical Bee, J*ournal of the History of Ideas* Vol. 22, No. 2 [Apr.-June, 1961]. The Johns Hopkins University Press.

4. Fraser, H.M. *Beekeeping in Antiquity.* University of London Press. London, 1951.

5. Style, Sue. *Honey From Hive to Honeypot*. Chronicle Books. San Francisco, CA, 1993.

6. More, Daphne, *The Bee Book : The History and Natural History of the Honeybee.* Universe Books. New York, 1976.

7. Gojmerac, Walter L. Bees, *Beekeeping, Honey and Pollination.* AVI Publishing Company, INC. Westport, Connecticut, 1980

8. Winston, Mark L. *The Biology of the Honey Bee*. Harvard University Press. Cambridge, Massachusetts, London, England, 1987.

9. Bonney, Richard E. *Beekeeping: A Practical Guide.* Storey Books. Pownal Vermont, 1993.

10. Free John Brand. *Bees and Mankind*. George Allen and Unwin publishers, London, 1982.

11. Teale, Edwin Way, *The Golden Throng*. Dodd, Mead & Company. New York, 1940.

12. Gould, James L., Gould, Carol Grant. *The Honey Bee*. Scientific American Library. New York, 1995.

10

The Existence of Sex in Plants

FRUITS ARE PAIRS

"AND FROM ALL the fruits He made pairs in double" [Surah 13: Verse 3].

"and sent down water from the sky with which We have produced pairs of various plants" [Surah 20: Verse 53].

This first Qur'anic verse refers to the existence of sex in fruits, which are flowering plants. Because the word "pair" in Arabic (*zawj*) may sometimes be interpreted as "the male being" of a couple, the word "in double" was possibly added to affirm the existence of two entities, *male and female*, forming a *pair*. The second verse refers to the fact that various plants, unlimited only to fruits, which emerge from the earth are also created as pairs.

Rickett defines fruits, from a botanist point of view, as "quite simply, are products of flowers" [1–163]. Flowers are the sexual organs of fruit producing plants, which are a highly advanced type of land plants, and flowers contain male and female parts [2–6]. The male component is known as stamens which produce pollen grains which fertilize the egg, producing what is known as the fertilized egg. The female component of the flower is known as the pistils which contain the ovary at the base along with the eggs and attract pollen grains [3-232 & Figure 1]. When the egg is fertilized, it is transformed into embryo, which is surrounded by large amount of stored food and protective coats and are collectively known as the "seed." The ovary itself transforms into the fruit which envelopes the seed, protects it and secures its dispersal [2–6].

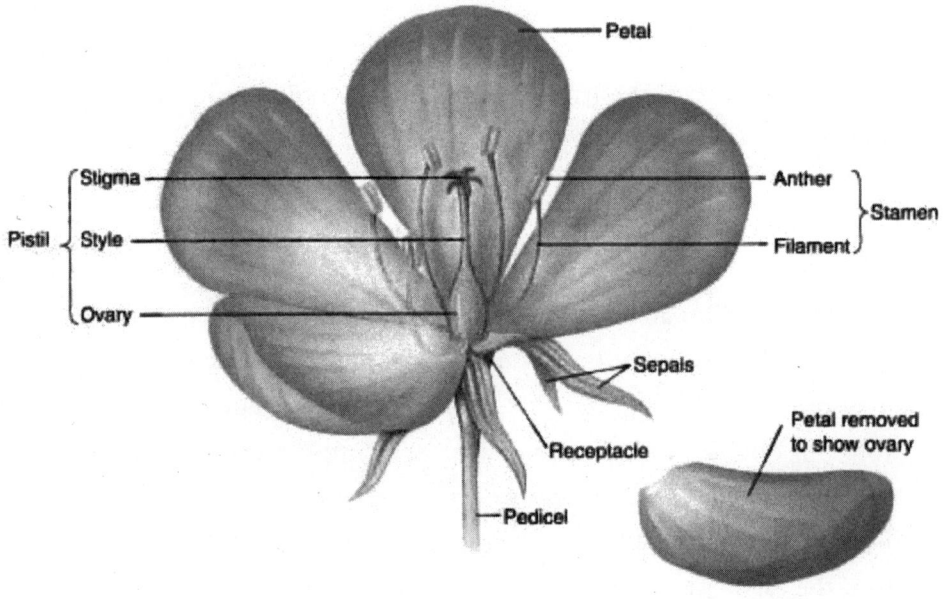

Figure 1:
The Flower, Sexual Components

Mauseth, James D. *Botany:
An Introduction to Plant Biology*, 1998.
Jones & Bartlett Publisher, Inc. Sudbury, Mass.
(reprinted with permission)

The male and female components of flowers commonly coexist in the same flower but may be located on different flowers and sometimes on different plants. When a flower is fertilized by pollen originating from the same flower or another flower on the same plant, fertilization is known as self pollination. When a flower is fertilized by pollen originating from another plant, fertilization is known as cross-pollination [3-247]. Mauseth relates that whereas no one mammal ever has both sperm producing organs and egg producing organs, almost all plants do have two types of spore producing organs [3-232].

Examining the ancient writings on the existence of sexuality in plants goes back to Aristotle in the fourth century B.C. who denied that sex existed among plants [4-57]. It was stated that the Roman author Pliny the elder in the first century A.D. seems to have recognized the existence of sex in plants, herbs as well as trees, but he only cited the old example of the date--palm and added no other observations of his own [4-74]. The date palm has a unique type of flower for, unlike common flowers, it contains only male or female organs (either stamens or pistils) and each kind grows on a different tree [1-149]. There are descriptions in ancient writings of the "artificial fertilization" of this tree as "the males should be brought to the females for the male makes them ripen and persist "by "shaking the dust from the male flower over the female" [5-52]. Singer thought that Pliny comments sounded very modern but examination of passages in ancient writings shows that the so-called "males" and "females" were "usually different species, and in some cases a sterile variety is described as the male and a fertile variety as the female" [5-51].

Albertus, the German philosopher and botanist of the 13th century believed, in his botanical work named "De Vegetabilibus," that sex, among other things, such as feeling, will and sleep do not exist in plants [4–105]. Caesalpinus, the Italian botanist and physiologist of the 16th century, who produced the first classification of plants according to their fruits, denied the existence of sex in plants [4–185]. Malpighi, the Italian anatomist who was the first to use a microscope in the study of anatomy, opposed the existence of sex in flowers and advocated the concept of spontaneous generation originally attributed to Aristotle [5–508]. Tournefort who described 10,146 plant species under 698 genera in 1694 expressly rejected the existence of sex in plants [4–240]. Hawks believes that Alston, who was professor of Botany at Edinburgh and died in 1760, was one of the last opponents of the existence of sex in plants [4–257].

The recognition by Grew and Ray of the universality of sex among flowering plants was especially significant, according to Hawks, as being a distinct contrary to previous thinking [4–220]. The definitive experimental evidence which proved this conclusion belongs to Camerarius whose observations were published in the latter part of the 17th century. He was able to demonstrate, by experiments, in the case of berries, that the fruits were seedless when no male specimen was in the vicinity. He isolated two female specimens and noted they grew seedless, in contrast to those who were among male plants [6–95]. Reed noted that "the process of fertilization was more correctly explained than ever before" [6–96]. Camerarius had also made the specific definition of male and female organs in the plants he studied.

Rickett, in 1943, wrote that the process of reproduction was poorly understood that "it was long thought that the pollen developed into the seed and that the pistils were a sort of nutritive receptacle for its development. This was still being taught in universities less than a hundred years ago." He added that "various learned societies in Europe offered prizes for demonstrations that pollen and pistils both contributed to the next generation ,that a plant actually had two parents" [1–149].

The Qur'an, here, affirms the existence of sex in plants, and unlike ancient writers, does not limit its scope to the date-palm or to only those visibly fertile plants, but extends the scope to all fruits and other plants. This was long before scientists and botanists, almost up to the 17th century, opposed the entire concept, and long before learned societies in Europe offered rewards for proving that *a plant does have two parents.*

THE ROLE OF THE WIND

"and We had sent the winds as fertilizers" [Surah 15: Verse 22].

After Camerarius experiments became established, the role of the wind as pollinator was specifically addressed in the 18th century by James Logan who was governor of Pennsylvania. He separated plants of corn at opposite ends of a plot of ground, about 80 feet apart, and noted "one large ear which grew out somewhat further from the stalk than usual and on that side which faced another hillock in a quarter from which our strongest winds most commonly blew" [6–96]. Reed noted that it thus appears that James Logan may be credited with the first appreciation of wind pollination about the year 1739 [6–96].

When pollination by the wind takes place, Mauseth explains, large numbers of pollen grains must be produced to enhance the chance of becoming engaged with a female organ of the flower. Seeds carried by the wind may become widely scattered and germinate in numerous diverse sites [3–230]. Wind is not the only effective pollinator to plants. Insects, attracted by sweet nectar or protein rich pollen transfer pollen grains from one flower and deposit them within the female organs of another flower when visiting this flower, therefore facilitating the act of sexual fertilization [3–249].

Almost one thousand years before Logan discovered the role of the wind in pollination, a Qur'anic verse was revealed making the statement that "and We had sent the winds as fertilizers" [Surah 15: Verse 22). The word translated as "fertilizers" is in Arabic (*Lawakeh*) which is a plura of the word (*Lukah*). *The Arabic English Dictionary* translates the word (*Lukah*) as "vaccine, inoculum" and the word (*Lakkaha*) which is the verb of the original word as "to pollinate, to fertilize" [7–346].

REFERENCES

1. Rickett, Harold William. *The Green Earth: An invitation to Botany.* Jacques Cattell Press. Lancaster, PA, 1943.

2. Hylander, Clarence J. *The World of Plant Life.* The Macmillan Company. New York, 1939.

3. Mauseth, James D. *Botany: An Introduction to Planet Biology.* Jones & Bartlett Publisher, Inc. Boston, 1998.

4. Hawks, Ellison. *Pioneers of Planet Study.* The Sheldon Press. London, 1928.

5. Singer, Charles. *A History of Biology to about the Year 1900: A General Introduction to the Study of Living Things.* Abelard-Schuman. London, 1959.

6. Reed S., Howard. *A Short History of the Plant Sciences*. Chronica Botanica Company. Waltham, MA, 1942.

7. Baalbaki, R.Al Mawred Al Quareeb--*Arabic English dictionary.* Dar El Elm Lilmalayin. Beirut, Lebanon, 2001.

76 Is The Qur'an God's Word?

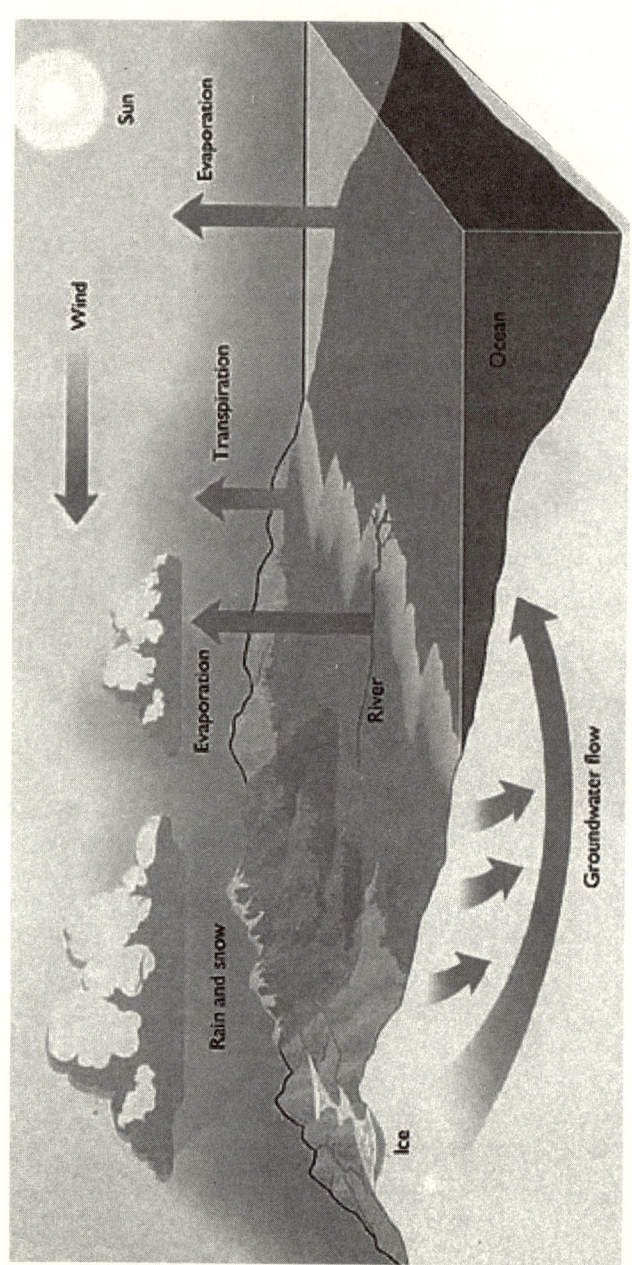

Figure 1: *The Hydrologic Cycle and Rain Formation*

Pinet, Paul R. *Invitation to Oceanography*, 1997. Jones & Bartlett Publishers, Inc. Sudbury. Mass. (reprinted with permission).

11

Rainfall

FORMATION OF CLOUDS AND RAINFALL

"GOD IS THE ONE Who sends the winds which raise clouds and He spreads them as He wills....then you see the rain drops from their midst" [Surah 30: Verse 48].

"and God is the one Who sends the winds which raise up clouds and then We direct them to a dead land so We may revive the earth after its death" [Surah 35: Verse 9].

"and God is the one Who sends the winds as heralds of His mercy so when they lead heavy clouds We direct them to a dead land so by them We descend down rain so We may produce by it all types of fruits" [Surah 7: Verse 57].

How clouds are formed and how rain falls?

The air and the atmosphere contain particles such as sea salt, air pollutants, smoke and dust. These particles are known as "the building blocks of clouds" [1–6].

Water vapor formed by evaporation of water by the effect of the sun, mainly from the surface of the ocean and to less extent from other bodies of water, rises upward which promotes cooling and subsequent condensation of water vapor around these air particles [2–163].

Clouds begin forming when progressive condensation leads to formation of cloud droplets, which are relatively small droplets ranging in size from 10 to 20 microns in diameter. As these droplets grow larger, usually to a diameter greater than 100 micron, they are called raindrops [1–23]. Mele et al indicate that when raindrops become "heavy enough," they fall as rain [2–163]. The heavier the raindrops are, the faster their descent is and the more likelihood they would reach the ground as rain [1–24].

Why is the repeated emphasis on the role of the wind in the Qur'an?

John Aitken, in 1880, discovered, for the first time, that condensation in the form of cloud, rain or fog requires the presence of particles in the atmosphere such as sea salt and other substances (also called nuclei) [3– 386]. He had shown that water vapor condense on these nuclei which act as the building blocks for cloud droplets [1–11]. The ocean is the chief source of salt nuclei [1–21]. Alfred Woodcock, in 1949, made observations over the ocean under many different conditions and found that, in general, the higher the wind velocity the greater the concentrations of nuclei in the atmosphere [1–21]. Also, the wind in blowing over the ocean moves water vapor, which results from the effect of the sun, up from the surface into the air. Then, water vapor is distributed over the land by the wind and the processes that lead to precipitation [4–304]. The form and motion of the clouds are related to the speed of air currents (winds) that are transporting the water droplets [5–204] & [Figure1]. Rain droplets fall to the ground when they become "heavy enough" [2–163].

How these Qur'anic verses conform to the scientific process of ordinary cloud and rain formation?

– These verses give a central role for the wind in provoking and initiating the process of cloud formation. This is now known to be accomplished by the wind increasing the number of nuclei in the atmosphere and driving water vapor upward for condensation. [all three verses].

— Subsequent condensation of water vapor over the atmospheric nuclei initiate the process of cloud formation with the motion and direction of the clouds being related to the speed of the wind [Surah 30: Verse 48 & Surah 35: Verse 9].

— When these clouds grow larger and their droplets attain a size which is "heavy" enough, they fall to the ground in the form or rain [Surah 7: Verse 57].

GROUND WATER

"We send down water from the sky, in measured amount, so We lodge it in the ground ....with it We grow for you gardens of date-palm and vines in them you have abundant fruits from which you eat" [Surah 23: Verse 18-19].

"do not you notice that God had sent down water from the sky and led it as springs in the earth" [Surah 39: Verse 21].

"do you see that if your water become lost deep in the underground who can then supply you with head-spring water?" [Surah 67: Verse 30].

It was thought in the past that the earth was impervious to allow the percolation of rainwater into the soil and rocks, from which it can reemerge in the form of springs [6–126]. Another prevalent notion was that the rainfall over the land was insufficient to supply the great quantities of water flowing into springs and rivers [7–460]. Adams explains that in early times, there has not been any knowledge of the size and extent of the oceans and the great volume of water vapor which could be raised from their surface by evaporation which subsequently falls as precipitation over the land [7–460].

Bernard Palissy who lived in the 16th century was among the earliest, if not indeed the first, to recognize and insist that rain and melting snow was the only source from which springs and rivers derive their waters [7–446]. The first experimental evidence to confirm this concept was the work of Pierre Perrault [1608 – 1680] who measured the drainage area of the Seine river near Paris from its source to a specific location and then made measurements of the annual rainfall over that area for three consecutive years [7–449]. He found that the amount of water flow through the river basin was equal to only about one sixth of the total rainfall over that area. He then concluded that the amount of rainfall over the area was clearly sufficient to act as a source of the water in the river [7– 449]. A few years later, Mariotte made measurements on the same river, using a larger area of the river and reached the same conclusion [7– 449]. Edmund Halley, in his observations on the Mediterranean Sea and its nine major rivers which were published in 1691, made a similar conclusion [8–33].

Gilluly observed that the flow of water in the major streams of practically all countries has been accurately determined by stream gauging. Also, rates of underground percolation of water and the amount of water stored in underground reservoirs have been measured from thousands of observations on springs and wells [6–127]. Adams concluded that the problem of the origin of springs and rivers may now be considered as definitely established; that these all have their origin in water precipitation on the earth surface [7–459].

Gilluly outlined the current concepts of distribution of precipitation which falls on the ground in the form of rain or snow. It is to be distributed within specific pathways. Some would seep into the soil and rock where would be temporarily stored underground. Some would be delivered to the roots of growing plants, and some would reemerge to the surface appearing in springs or streams [6–127] & [Figure 1]. Brauer related that ultimately a great river reaches the sea [9–56].

REFERENCES

1. Battan, Louis J. *The Cloud Physics and Cloud Seeding*. Anchor Books. Garden City, NY, 1962.

2. Mele, Frank Michael, Navarra John Gabriel, Weisberg, Joseph S. *Earth Science*. Wiley. New York, 1971.

3. Bentley, Wilson A, Humphreys, W.J. *Ways of the Weather: A Cultural Survey of Meteorology.* The Jaques Cattell Press. Lancaster, PA, 1943.

4. King, Cuchlaine A.M. *An Introduction to Oceanography.* McGrawHill. New York, 1963.

5. Pinet, Paul R. *Invitation to Oceanography.* Sudbury, Mass. Jones & Barlett Publishers, Inc. Sudbury, Mass. 1997.

6. Gilluly, James. *Principles of Geology*. W.H. Freeman. San Francisco, 1958.

7. Adams, Frank Dawson. *The Birth and Development of the Geological Sciences*. Dover Publications. New York, 1954.

8. Wallace, William J. *The Development of the Chlorinity / Salinity Concept in Oceanography.* Elsevier Scientific Publishing Company. Amsterdam, 1974.

9. Brauer, Billy. Water: *A Natural History.* Basic Books. New York, 1996.

12

Where The Seas Meet

THE TWO SEAS

VERSE No. 1: "He laid down the two seas meeting together, between them is a separation zone which they do not transgress" [Surah 55: Verses 19–20].

The word translated here as "separation zone" is in Arabic "*barzakh*," which precisely means a separation or transitional zone between two specific entities.

The only other place in the Qur'an where this word was used, with no relationship to the seas, is in verse Surah 23: Verse 100: "and behind them is a transition zone '*barzakh*' till the day they are raised up." This is a reference to a separation, either in space or in time, which separates the end of a person's life on Earth from the day he is to be raised up (day of resurrection). Many Qur'anic commentators, based on this verse, speculated that there might be some type of transitional spiritual life inter-positioned between the two lives, which they called (the life of the "*barzakh*").

A synonym to the word "transgress" in Arabic is "unfairly predominates," meaning that neither of the two seas "unfairly predominates " over the other.

Each of two adjacent seas has its own distinctive physical, chemical and biological features but a "separation zone" between two seas has specific flow patterns, which are intended to accomplish specific goals. We will refer here to two examples from the Mediterranean Sea, the Black Sea and the Atlantic Ocean.

(A) The Case of the Mediterranean Sea and the Atlantic Ocean

In the Mediterranean Sea, due to its dominant hot and dry climate, evaporation, in general, exceeds the combined effects of precipitation and river inflow, therefore, the water of the Mediterranean is saltier and warmer than that of the Atlantic Ocean and has a higher density [1–202]. Consequently, the sea surface is lower than that of the Atlantic Ocean, therefore, surface water from the Atlantic flows into the Mediterranean across the strait of Gibraltar [2–220]. The strait of Gibraltar is approximately 58 kilometers long, and separates Africa from Europe at the Western end of the Mediterranean. Conversely, the deep dense warm water of the Mediterranean flows across the strait and spreads out horizontally into

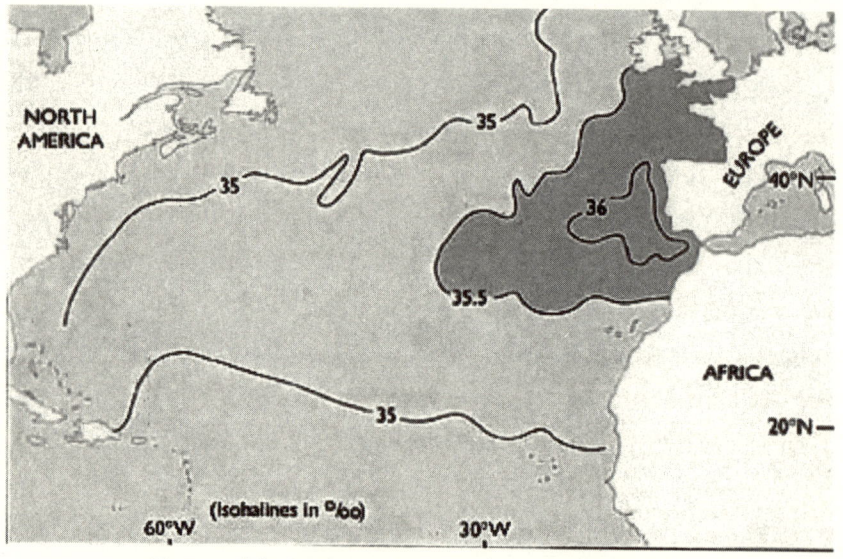

Figure 1: The Mediterranean Sea & the Atlantic Ocean:

Salinity at a depth of 1,000 meters shows the distribution of the Mediterranean water in the North Atlantic. A similar illustration made for temperature variations also shows the same distribution pattern. Pinet, Paul R. *Invitation to Oceanography,* 1997. Jones & Bartlett Publishers, Inc. Sudbury, Mass. (reprinted with permission).

the Atlantic Ocean at mid depth forming a distinct water mass [1–203] & [Figure1]. This water mass extends horizontally thousands of kilometers from its point of origin, and can be distinguished by its specific characteristics which are those of the Mediterranean salinity and temperature[1–207].

We should keep in mind that although the salinity of the incoming surface water from the Atlantic could slightly rise when immediately blended with the Mediterranean water and flowing eastward, the deep Mediterranean water throughout maintains its characteristic salinity between 38.4 to 39 and increases to 40 in the eastern Mediterranean basin as well as its characteristic temperature between 12.5°C to 13.5°C in the west and 13.5°C to 15°C n the eastern Mediterranean [2 – 212& 221].

(B) The Case of the Black Sea and the Mediterranean:
The Black Sea has a connection to the Mediterranean Sea through the Bosporus strait which has a length of approximately 31 kilometers and ends at the Sea of Marmara which connects with the Mediterranean [2--256]. Conditions In the Black Sea are opposite to the Mediterranean with precipitation and the river inflow exceeding the amount removed by evaporation ,therefore, the surface water in the Black Sea shows low density and diluted salinity [1–208].

In order to discharge the excess water from the Black Sea produced by excess precipitation, the surface water which has a salinity of 17 to 18 per thousand flows from the Black Sea into the Sea of Marmara and subsequently into the Mediterranean [2–257]. The deep Mediterranean water, which has a density higher than the deep water of the Black Sea passes northeast through the Bosporus, with its distinct characteristics, as a deep thin layer of dense warm water into the Black Sea. Then the water changes directions after entering the

86　Is The Qur'an God's Word?

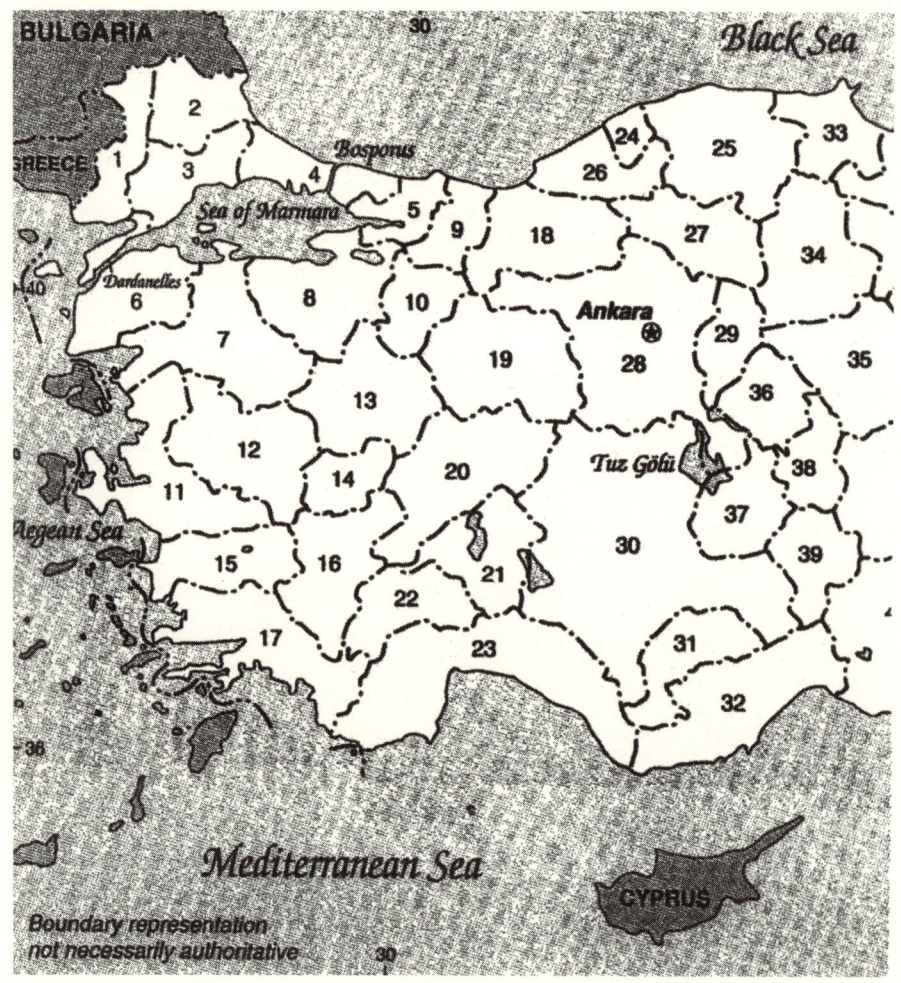

Figure 2:
Connection of the Black Sea and the Mediterranean Sea through the Bosporus strait and the Sea of Marmara

[Picture Credit: *Turkey, a Country Study.* Federal Research Division, United States government, 1996.]

Black Sea moving west – northwest as a thin layer of water with increased salinity extending up to about 50 kilometers from the Bosporus entrance [2–257] & [Figure 2]. About 20 species of Mediterranean zooplankton ride through the sea of Marmara and have been found in the Black Sea. Some of these species does not only survive but in fact multiply in the Black Sea [2–258].

Study of nature of the Black Sea were started by P. Pallas with his description of the fish populations in the late 18th century. Studies of the hydrology of the Black Sea were conducted by Admiral S. Makarov in 1880 and later in 1890 by a special deep sea expedition organized by two other scientists. Their studies identified the main features of the origin, morphometry, circulation, chemistry and zoogeography of the sea up to the beginning of the 20th century [2–254].

We should mention here that these distinct water masses, which act as separate or transitional zones between two adjacent seas, are not visible to the human eye, and that their identification requires detailed analysis of their specific physical and chemical characteristics as has been done in scientific missions of exploration of the seas, which we will review below.

Verse No. 2: "And He made between the two seas a barrier" [Surah 27: Verse 61]

Unlike the word used in verse No. 1 "*barzakh*", the word used in this verse "*Hajez*" means strictly a " barrier." "The barrier between the two seas" in this verse is a likely reference to adjacent interconnected seas which may appear as similar bodies of water, but each has its own specific distinguishing chemical, physical and biological features [2–210]. Other than in separation or transitional zones between seas (*barzakh*) which perform specific functions necessary for preservation of the features of each sea, characteristics such as water density, salinity, temperature and biota can be entirely different between two adjacent seas.

There is another important "barrier" among seas. Every "ocean", although interconnected with other oceans, exhibits its own chemical characteristics which would distinguish it from other oceans. W. T. Holsar, a geophysicist at the University of California asked "can different oceans be characterized by differences in chemical composition?. Richard H. Fleming, a leader in pioneering studies of the chemistry of the oceans [3–23], replied "yes. If a sample labeled only by depth is presented to a chemist, he can ,by analyzing chlorinity, calcium, alkalinity and nutrients, distinguish whether it is from the Atlantic, Pacific or Indian Oceans" [3–25, John Farrington].

The River and the Sea

VERSE No. 3: "He who set the two seas, this is palatable and sweet and this is salty and bitter and had created between them a separation and boundary which is well bounded" [Surah 25: Verse 53].

In this verse, the same word translated as "separation or transitional zone" which was used in verse No. 1 "*barzakh*" is repeated here for the case where a river meets the sea, but the description is further characterized as "a boundary which is well bounded." In this case, the reference is being made to the estuaries. Some Qur'anic commentators, as recently as the early part of the 20th century, likely unaware of the reference to the estuaries in this verse, assumed that the statements made here were symbolic. They interpreted the statements as "the fresh and sweet water as referring to God revelations and the salt and bitter water were referring to man worldly desires and motives" [4–939] or that God "can raise up a righteous community from among a large wicked society" [5–vol. 8, 198].

Ketchum described an estuary as a transition zone between the world of freshwater and the sea water offshore [2–1]. Estuaries have distinctive environments which result from the existence of two opposing current systems; the freshwater outflow and the sea tide inflow [6–69]. The mixing of salt water and freshwater produces a chemical environment unlike that of a typical sea or typical river [6–69]. Salinity increases horizontally from virtually zero in the river water to reach the salinity of the sea at coastal areas. Vertical variations in salinity also occur and these variations may become more pronounced according to the tide ebb and flow [2–1].

Living organisms, therefore, must possess various mechanisms in order to survive in such environment [2–1]. One significant biologic feature of estuaries is the presence of oyster reef which is an assemblage of an interesting community of various organisms usually found at the mouth of the estuaries [6–79].

From geologic standpoint, estuaries have unique features of erosion and deposition so there is a mixture of sand, mud and silt in various proportions and degrees of compaction [6–7/8]. Another typical feature is the existence of tidal marshes with salt marsh grading into freshwater marsh [6–80].

Therefore, an estuary in general, is a unique environment of physical, chemical, biologic and geologic features. This must be recognized if an estuary is to be described as "a separation or a transitional zone and a boundary which is well bounded."

How our Knowledge of Sea Water Developed and Evolved?

Ancient writers and philosophers, mainly Greeks, made speculations about the possible origins of salt in the sea, but nothing of practical value emerged with respect to sea water studies till the time of Robert Boyle. Robert Boyle [1627–1691] in his "Observations and

Experiments about the Saltness of the Sea" designed a scheme for analysis of natural water as well as salt water of the sea [7–23]. He developed his information from his own experiments as well as from interviews with mariners, which established him as "the father of the science known now as chemical oceanography." He however thought that the sea was as salty from the top to bottom and there was no difference in general in the surface and bottom saltness from one place to another. He obtained deep water samples but these samples were apparently not deep enough, never from deeper than a few meters [7–28].

The Swedish scientist T.O. Bergman [1735–1784] developed a quantitative and qualitative scheme for analyzing natural waters [7–49]. Then, he began analysis of sea water and was able to determine salinity as well as alkalinity and other elements in sea water, using the evaporation and precipitation techniques [7–52].

Forchhammer devised the term salinity in the 19th century as a description of the degree of saltness of the sea. In 1899, the Swedish Hydrographic Commission devised an equation to calculate the salinity. Salinity is one of three parameters used to calculate the "density" along with temperature and pressure [7–Preface]. Salinity and density calculation is essential for identifying the characteristics of specific water masses [7–Preface].

Aside from sea water analysis, scientific exploration of the vast oceans began with Capt. James Cook in his three Pacific expeditions between 1768 and 1779 [8–18]. At that time, most of the globe was unexplored and maps were drawn from imagination as well as from experience [8–18]. James Cook was able to map much of the Pacific Ocean shoreline [8–18].

The first expedition undertaken purely for scientific reasons was the voyage of the HMS Challenger from 1872 to 1876 directed by Charles W Thomson [9 –19] which set out to investigate "everything about the sea" [8–18]. The Challenger completed a globe encircling voyage covering almost 125,000 kilometers or 77,500 miles [1–19]. The researchers, stopping every two hundred miles, made physical, chemical, biological, and geological measurements in all the oceans except the Arctic [8–18]. The Meteor expedition to the South Atlantic Ocean took place between 1925 and 1927, by German scientists, used highly developed oceanographic equipment to complete an unprecedented survey of the ocean and gather vertical profiles of salinity, water temperature and dissolved oxygen at numerous stations [1– 20]. No data of such quality had ever before been gathered from the ocean [1–20].

John Farrington related that the importance of knowing the density of seawater drove a significant part of chemical oceanography ,during the period of 1900 to 1950, to focus on salinity measurement or surrogates such as chlorinity and to affirm the ratio of major chemicals in various sea waters [3–24]. This was the beginning for understanding the distinctive chemical features of distinctive water masses [3–24].

With accumulation of this knowledge at hand, it became possible to identify specific characteristics of every sea and ocean, to identify the characteristics of any separation or transitional zones among adjacent seas and to determine the true characteristics of the boundaries containing estuaries where a river meet the sea.

REFERENCES

1. Pinet, Paul R. *Invitation to Oceanography.* Jones & Bartlet Publishers, Inc. Sudbury, Mass., 1997.

2. Ketchum, Bostwick, H (including :Miller, A & Sorokin,Y.I). *Estuaries and the Enclosed Seas.* Elsevier Scientific Publishing Company. Amsterdam, 1983.

3. Farrington John in: *50 Years of Ocean Discovery*: National Science Foundation, 1950-2000. National Academy Press. Washington DC, 2000.

4. Ali A Yusuf. *The Meaning of The Holy Qur'an*, Amana Corporation. Maryland, 1983.

5. Abu Ala Maududi. *The Meaning of The Qur'an*, vol. 8. Islamic Publications [Pvt] Ltd.. Lahore, 1979.

6. Reid, George K. *Ecology of Inland Waters and Estuaries.* Reinhold. New York, 1961

7. Wallace, William J. *The Development of the Chlorinity / Salinity Concept in Oceanography.* Elsevier Scientific Publishing Company. Amsterdam, 1974.

8. *Exploration of the Seas: Voyage Into the Unknown.* National Academies Press. Washington, DC, 2003.

9. Reddy, M.P.M.*Descriptive Physical Oceanography.* Swets & Zeitlinger. Lisse [Netherlands], Extons, PA, 2001

13

Two More Observations

OBSERVATION 1: "He merges the night into the day and merges the day into the night" [Surah 31: Verse 29].

"He encircles the night over the day and encircles the day over the night" [Surah 39: Verse 5].

The first verse is a simple reference to the phenomena of the dawn and the sunset and needs no further elaboration. The second verse deserves special attention. The word "*ukaweru*" in Arabic means to encircle, or to coil or to make something in the form of a ball. The original reference word for this verb is "*kurah*" which means "ball."

OBSERVATION 2: "He is Who created the night and the day and the sun and the moon each is swimming in a rounded course" [Surah 21: Verse 33].

This verse describes the circular motion of the sun and moon, which is visible to humans as a natural phenomenon and again needs no further explanation. What deserves special attention is the reference to the night and the day as moving into a circular motion as evident by the word "each," which included each of the four entities listed in the verse.

I do not wish to make any further comments about these two verses. They would be left up to the reader's own speculations.

The Qur'anic Verses in Arabic

Chapter 1
The Universe: Landmarks of the Creation

$$\text{﴿٣٠﴾ أَوَلَمْ يَرَ الَّذِينَ كَفَرُوا أَنَّ السَّمَاوَاتِ وَالْأَرْضَ كَانَتَا رَتْقًا فَفَتَقْنَاهُمَا وَجَعَلْنَا مِنَ الْمَاءِ كُلَّ شَيْءٍ حَيٍّ أَفَلَا يُؤْمِنُونَ}$$

[Surah 21: Verse 30]

$$\text{﴿١١﴾ ثُمَّ اسْتَوَىٰ إِلَى السَّمَاءِ وَهِيَ دُخَانٌ فَقَالَ لَهَا وَلِلْأَرْضِ ائْتِيَا طَوْعًا أَوْ كَرْهًا قَالَتَا أَتَيْنَا طَائِعِينَ}$$

[Surah 41: Verse 11]

$$\text{﴿٤٧﴾ وَالسَّمَاءَ بَنَيْنَاهَا بِأَيْدٍ وَإِنَّا لَمُوسِعُونَ}$$

[Surah 51: Verse 47]

وَلَوْ فَتَحْنَا عَلَيْهِم بَابًا مِّنَ ٱلسَّمَاءِ فَظَلُّوا۟ فِيهِ يَعْرُجُونَ ﴿١٤﴾ [Surah 15: Verse 14]

تَعْرُجُ ٱلْمَلَٰٓئِكَةُ وَٱلرُّوحُ إِلَيْهِ فِى يَوْمٍ كَانَ مِقْدَارُهُۥ خَمْسِينَ أَلْفَ سَنَةٍ ﴿٤﴾ [Surah 70: Verse 4]

يَوْمَ نَطْوِى ٱلسَّمَآءَ كَطَىِّ ٱلسِّجِلِّ لِلْكُتُبِ ۚ كَمَا بَدَأْنَآ أَوَّلَ خَلْقٍ نُّعِيدُهُۥ ۚ وَعْدًا عَلَيْنَآ ۚ إِنَّا كُنَّا فَٰعِلِينَ ﴿١٠٤﴾ [Surah 21: Verse 104]

Chapter 2
The Heavens & The Earth: Stages of the Creation

[Surah 50: Verse 38]

﴿٣٨﴾ وَلَقَدْ خَلَقْنَا ٱلسَّمَٰوَٰتِ وَٱلْأَرْضَ وَمَا بَيْنَهُمَا فِى سِتَّةِ أَيَّامٍ وَمَا مَسَّنَا مِن لُّغُوبٍ

[Surah 22: Verse 47]

﴿٤٧﴾ وَيَسْتَعْجِلُونَكَ بِٱلْعَذَابِ وَلَن يُخْلِفَ ٱللَّهُ وَعْدَهُۥ ۚ وَإِنَّ يَوْمًا عِندَ رَبِّكَ كَأَلْفِ سَنَةٍ مِّمَّا تَعُدُّونَ

[Surah 70: Verse 4]

﴿٤﴾ تَعْرُجُ ٱلْمَلَٰٓئِكَةُ وَٱلرُّوحُ إِلَيْهِ فِى يَوْمٍ كَانَ مِقْدَارُهُۥ خَمْسِينَ أَلْفَ سَنَةٍ

Is The Qur'an God's Word?

﴿٢٧﴾ ءَأَنتُمْ أَشَدُّ خَلْقًا أَمِ ٱلسَّمَاءُ بَنَىٰهَا

﴿٢٨﴾ رَفَعَ سَمْكَهَا فَسَوَّىٰهَا

﴿٢٩﴾ وَأَغْطَشَ لَيْلَهَا وَأَخْرَجَ ضُحَىٰهَا

﴿٣٠﴾ وَٱلْأَرْضَ بَعْدَ ذَٰلِكَ دَحَىٰهَا

﴿٣١﴾ أَخْرَجَ مِنْهَا مَآءَهَا وَمَرْعَىٰهَا

﴿٣٢﴾ وَٱلْجِبَالَ أَرْسَىٰهَا

[Surah 79: Verse 27–32]

﴿٩﴾ قُلْ أَئِنَّكُمْ لَتَكْفُرُونَ بِٱلَّذِى خَلَقَ ٱلْأَرْضَ فِى يَوْمَيْنِ

[Surah 41: Verse 9]

وَيَجْعَلُونَ لَهُۥ أَندَادًا
ذَٰلِكَ رَبُّ ٱلْعَٰلَمِينَ

﴿١٠﴾ وَجَعَلَ فِيهَا رَوَٰسِىَ
مِن فَوْقِهَا وَبَٰرَكَ فِيهَا
وَقَدَّرَ فِيهَآ أَقْوَٰتَهَا فِىٓ
أَرْبَعَةِ أَيَّامٍ سَوَآءً
لِّلسَّآئِلِينَ

﴿١١﴾ ثُمَّ ٱسْتَوَىٰٓ إِلَى ٱلسَّمَآءِ
وَهِىَ دُخَانٌ فَقَالَ لَهَا وَلِلْأَرْضِ
ٱئْتِيَا طَوْعًا أَوْ كَرْهًا
قَالَتَآ أَتَيْنَا طَآئِعِينَ

﴿١٢﴾ فَقَضَىٰهُنَّ سَبْعَ سَمَٰوَاتٍ
فِى يَوْمَيْنِ وَأَوْحَىٰ
فِى كُلِّ سَمَآءٍ أَمْرَهَا
وَزَيَّنَّا ٱلسَّمَآءَ ٱلدُّنْيَا
بِمَصَٰبِيحَ وَحِفْظًا
ذَٰلِكَ تَقْدِيرُ ٱلْعَزِيزِ ٱلْعَلِيمِ [Surah 41: Verse 10–12]

> ﴿٢٩﴾ هُوَ ٱلَّذِى خَلَقَ لَكُم مَّا فِى ٱلْأَرْضِ جَمِيعًا ثُمَّ ٱسْتَوَىٰٓ إِلَى ٱلسَّمَآءِ فَسَوَّىٰهُنَّ سَبْعَ سَمَٰوَٰتٍ وَهُوَ بِكُلِّ شَىْءٍ عَلِيمٌ

[Surah 2: Verse 29]

> ﴿٣﴾ ٱلَّذِى خَلَقَ سَبْعَ سَمَٰوَٰتٍ طِبَاقًا مَّا تَرَىٰ فِى خَلْقِ ٱلرَّحْمَٰنِ مِن تَفَٰوُتٍ فَٱرْجِعِ ٱلْبَصَرَ هَلْ تَرَىٰ مِن فُطُورٍ

[Surah 67: Verse 3]

Chapter 3
Ascension in The Sky

فَمَن يُرِدِ ٱللَّهُ أَن يَهْدِيَهُۥ يَشْرَحْ صَدْرَهُۥ لِلْإِسْلَٰمِ ۖ وَمَن يُرِدْ أَن يُضِلَّهُۥ يَجْعَلْ صَدْرَهُۥ ضَيِّقًا حَرَجًا كَأَنَّمَا يَصَّعَّدُ فِى ٱلسَّمَآءِ ۚ كَذَٰلِكَ يَجْعَلُ ٱللَّهُ ٱلرِّجْسَ عَلَى ٱلَّذِينَ لَا يُؤْمِنُونَ

[Surah 6: Verse 125]

Chapter 4
The Lowest Earth

﴿٢﴾ غُلِبَتِ ٱلرُّومُ

﴿٣﴾ فِىٓ أَدْنَى ٱلْأَرْضِ وَهُم مِّنۢ بَعْدِ غَلَبِهِمْ سَيَغْلِبُونَ

﴿٤﴾ فِى بِضْعِ سِنِينَ ۗ لِلَّهِ ٱلْأَمْرُ مِن قَبْلُ وَمِنۢ بَعْدُ ۚ وَيَوْمَئِذٍ يَفْرَحُ ٱلْمُؤْمِنُونَ

[Surah 30: Verse 2–4]

Chapter 5
The Descended Iron

۞ لَقَدْ أَرْسَلْنَا رُسُلَنَا بِٱلْبَيِّنَٰتِ وَأَنزَلْنَا مَعَهُمُ ٱلْكِتَٰبَ وَٱلْمِيزَانَ لِيَقُومَ ٱلنَّاسُ بِٱلْقِسْطِ ۖ وَأَنزَلْنَا ٱلْحَدِيدَ فِيهِ بَأْسٌ شَدِيدٌ وَمَنَٰفِعُ لِلنَّاسِ وَلِيَعْلَمَ ٱللَّهُ مَن يَنصُرُهُۥ وَرُسُلَهُۥ بِٱلْغَيْبِ ۚ إِنَّ ٱللَّهَ قَوِيٌّ عَزِيزٌ

[Surah 57 : Verse 25]

Chapter 6
Mountains are Pegs

وَٱلْجِبَالَ أَوْتَادًا ﴿٧﴾   [Surah 78: Verse 7]

Chapter 7
Human Reproduction

[Surah 76: Verse 2]

$$\text{إِنَّا خَلَقْنَا الْإِنسَانَ مِن نُّطْفَةٍ أَمْشَاجٍ نَّبْتَلِيهِ فَجَعَلْنَاهُ سَمِيعًا بَصِيرًا}$$

[Surah 96: Verse 2]

$$\text{خَلَقَ الْإِنسَانَ مِنْ عَلَقٍ}$$

[Surah 23: Verse 14]

$$\text{ثُمَّ خَلَقْنَا النُّطْفَةَ عَلَقَةً فَخَلَقْنَا الْعَلَقَةَ مُضْغَةً فَخَلَقْنَا الْمُضْغَةَ عِظَامًا فَكَسَوْنَا الْعِظَامَ لَحْمًا ثُمَّ أَنشَأْنَاهُ خَلْقًا آخَرَ فَتَبَارَكَ اللَّهُ أَحْسَنُ الْخَالِقِينَ}$$

يَٰٓأَيُّهَا ٱلنَّاسُ إِن كُنتُمْ فِى رَيْبٍ مِّنَ ٱلْبَعْثِ فَإِنَّا خَلَقْنَٰكُم مِّن تُرَابٍ ثُمَّ مِن نُّطْفَةٍ ثُمَّ مِنْ عَلَقَةٍ ثُمَّ مِن مُّضْغَةٍ مُّخَلَّقَةٍ وَغَيْرِ مُخَلَّقَةٍ لِّنُبَيِّنَ لَكُمْ ۚ وَنُقِرُّ فِى ٱلْأَرْحَامِ مَا نَشَآءُ إِلَىٰٓ أَجَلٍ مُّسَمًّى ثُمَّ نُخْرِجُكُمْ طِفْلًا ثُمَّ لِتَبْلُغُوٓا۟ أَشُدَّكُمْ ۖ وَمِنكُم مَّن يُتَوَفَّىٰ وَمِنكُم مَّن يُرَدُّ إِلَىٰٓ أَرْذَلِ ٱلْعُمُرِ لِكَيْلَا يَعْلَمَ مِنۢ بَعْدِ عِلْمٍ شَيْـًٔا ۚ وَتَرَى ٱلْأَرْضَ هَامِدَةً فَإِذَآ أَنزَلْنَا عَلَيْهَا ٱلْمَآءَ ٱهْتَزَّتْ وَرَبَتْ وَأَنۢبَتَتْ مِن كُلِّ زَوْجٍۭ بَهِيجٍ

[Surah 22: Verse 5]

أَلَمْ يَكُ نُطْفَةً مِّن مَّنِىٍّ يُمْنَىٰ ۝

[Surah 75: Verse 37]

Chapter 8
Water in the Living Organism

﴿٣٠﴾ أَوَلَمْ يَرَ الَّذِينَ كَفَرُوا أَنَّ السَّمَاوَاتِ وَالْأَرْضَ كَانَتَا رَتْقًا فَفَتَقْنَاهُمَا وَجَعَلْنَا مِنَ الْمَاءِ كُلَّ شَيْءٍ حَيٍّ أَفَلَا يُؤْمِنُونَ

[Surah 21: Verse 30]

﴿٤٥﴾ وَاللَّهُ خَلَقَ كُلَّ دَابَّةٍ مِّن مَّاءٍ فَمِنْهُم مَّن يَمْشِي عَلَىٰ بَطْنِهِ وَمِنْهُم مَّن يَمْشِي عَلَىٰ رِجْلَيْنِ وَمِنْهُم مَّن يَمْشِي عَلَىٰ أَرْبَعٍ يَخْلُقُ اللَّهُ مَا يَشَاءُ إِنَّ اللَّهَ عَلَىٰ كُلِّ شَيْءٍ قَدِيرٌ

[Surah 24: Verse 45]

Chapter 9
Qur'anic Comments on the Honeybee

﴿٦٨﴾ وَأَوْحَىٰ رَبُّكَ إِلَى ٱلنَّحْلِ أَنِ ٱتَّخِذِي مِنَ ٱلْجِبَالِ بُيُوتًا وَمِنَ ٱلشَّجَرِ وَمِمَّا يَعْرِشُونَ

﴿٦٩﴾ ثُمَّ كُلِي مِن كُلِّ ٱلثَّمَرَٰتِ فَٱسْلُكِي سُبُلَ رَبِّكِ ذُلُلًا ۚ يَخْرُجُ مِنۢ بُطُونِهَا شَرَابٌ مُّخْتَلِفٌ أَلْوَٰنُهُۥ فِيهِ شِفَآءٌ لِّلنَّاسِ ۗ إِنَّ فِى ذَٰلِكَ لَءَايَةً لِّقَوْمٍ يَتَفَكَّرُونَ

[Surah 16: Verse 68–69]

Chapter 10
The Existence of Sex in Plants

وَهُوَ الَّذِي مَدَّ الْأَرْضَ وَجَعَلَ فِيهَا رَوَاسِيَ وَأَنْهَارًا وَمِن كُلِّ الثَّمَرَاتِ جَعَلَ فِيهَا زَوْجَيْنِ اثْنَيْنِ يُغْشِي اللَّيْلَ النَّهَارَ إِنَّ فِي ذَٰلِكَ لَآيَاتٍ لِّقَوْمٍ يَتَفَكَّرُونَ

[Surah 13: Verse 3]

الَّذِي جَعَلَ لَكُمُ الْأَرْضَ مَهْدًا وَسَلَكَ لَكُمْ فِيهَا سُبُلًا وَأَنزَلَ مِنَ السَّمَاءِ مَاءً فَأَخْرَجْنَا بِهِ أَزْوَاجًا مِّن نَّبَاتٍ شَتَّىٰ

[Surah 20: Verse 53]

وَأَرْسَلْنَا الرِّيَاحَ لَوَاقِحَ فَأَنزَلْنَا مِنَ السَّمَاءِ مَاءً فَأَسْقَيْنَاكُمُوهُ وَمَا أَنتُمْ لَهُ بِخَازِنِينَ

[Surah 15: Verse 22]

Chapter 11
Rainfall

﴿٤٨﴾ ٱللَّهُ ٱلَّذِى يُرْسِلُ ٱلرِّيَـٰحَ فَتُثِيرُ سَحَابًا فَيَبْسُطُهُۥ فِى ٱلسَّمَآءِ كَيْفَ يَشَآءُ وَيَجْعَلُهُۥ كِسَفًا فَتَرَى ٱلْوَدْقَ يَخْرُجُ مِنْ خِلَـٰلِهِۦ فَإِذَآ أَصَابَ بِهِۦ مَن يَشَآءُ مِنْ عِبَادِهِۦٓ إِذَا هُمْ يَسْتَبْشِرُونَ

[Surah 30: Verse 48]

﴿٩﴾ وَٱللَّهُ ٱلَّذِىٓ أَرْسَلَ ٱلرِّيَـٰحَ فَتُثِيرُ سَحَابًا فَسُقْنَـٰهُ إِلَىٰ بَلَدٍ مَّيِّتٍ فَأَحْيَيْنَا بِهِ ٱلْأَرْضَ بَعْدَ مَوْتِهَا كَذَٰلِكَ ٱلنُّشُورُ

[Surah 35: Verse 9]

> ۝ وَهُوَ ٱلَّذِى يُرْسِلُ ٱلرِّيَٰحَ بُشْرًۢا بَيْنَ يَدَىْ رَحْمَتِهِۦ ۖ حَتَّىٰٓ إِذَآ أَقَلَّتْ سَحَابًا ثِقَالًا سُقْنَٰهُ لِبَلَدٍ مَّيِّتٍ فَأَنزَلْنَا بِهِ ٱلْمَآءَ فَأَخْرَجْنَا بِهِۦ مِن كُلِّ ٱلثَّمَرَٰتِ ۚ كَذَٰلِكَ نُخْرِجُ ٱلْمَوْتَىٰ لَعَلَّكُمْ تَذَكَّرُونَ

[Surah 7: Verse 57]

> ۝ وَلَقَدْ خَلَقْنَا فَوْقَكُمْ سَبْعَ طَرَآئِقَ
> فَأَسْكَنَّٰهُ فِى ٱلْأَرْضِ ۖ وَإِنَّا عَلَىٰ ذَهَابٍۭ بِهِۦ لَقَٰدِرُونَ
>
> ۝ فَأَنشَأْنَا لَكُم بِهِۦ جَنَّٰتٍ مِّن نَّخِيلٍ وَأَعْنَٰبٍ لَّكُمْ فِيهَا فَوَٰكِهُ كَثِيرَةٌ وَمِنْهَا تَأْكُلُونَ

[Surah 23: Verse 18-19]

أَلَمْ تَرَ أَنَّ ٱللَّهَ أَنزَلَ مِنَ ٱلسَّمَاءِ مَاءً فَسَلَكَهُۥ يَنَٰبِيعَ فِى ٱلْأَرْضِ ثُمَّ يُخْرِجُ بِهِۦ زَرْعًا مُّخْتَلِفًا أَلْوَٰنُهُۥ ثُمَّ يَهِيجُ فَتَرَىٰهُ مُصْفَرًّا ثُمَّ يَجْعَلُهُۥ حُطَٰمًا ۚ إِنَّ فِى ذَٰلِكَ لَذِكْرَىٰ لِأُو۟لِى ٱلْأَلْبَٰبِ

[Surah 39: Verse 21]

قُلْ أَرَءَيْتُمْ إِنْ أَصْبَحَ مَآؤُكُمْ غَوْرًا فَمَن يَأْتِيكُم بِمَآءٍ مَّعِينٍۭ

[Surah 67: Verse 30]

The Qur'anic Verses in Arabic

Chapter 12
Where The Seas Meet

﴿١٩﴾ مَرَجَ ٱلْبَحْرَيْنِ يَلْتَقِيَانِ

﴿٢٠﴾ بَيْنَهُمَا بَرْزَخٌ لَّا يَبْغِيَانِ   [Surah 55: Verse 19–20]

﴿١٠٠﴾ لَعَلِّي أَعْمَلُ صَٰلِحًا فِيمَا تَرَكْتُ ۚ كَلَّا ۚ إِنَّهَا كَلِمَةٌ هُوَ قَآئِلُهَا ۖ وَمِن وَرَآئِهِم بَرْزَخٌ إِلَىٰ يَوْمِ يُبْعَثُونَ

[Surah 23: Verse 100]

أَمَّن جَعَلَ ٱلْأَرْضَ قَرَارًا وَجَعَلَ خِلَٰلَهَآ أَنْهَٰرًا وَجَعَلَ لَهَا رَوَاسِىَ وَجَعَلَ بَيْنَ ٱلْبَحْرَيْنِ حَاجِزًا ۗ أَءِلَٰهٌ مَّعَ ٱللَّهِ ۚ بَلْ أَكْثَرُهُمْ لَا يَعْلَمُونَ

[Surah 27: Verse 61]

وَهُوَ ٱلَّذِى مَرَجَ ٱلْبَحْرَيْنِ هَٰذَا عَذْبٌ فُرَاتٌ وَهَٰذَا مِلْحٌ أُجَاجٌ وَجَعَلَ بَيْنَهُمَا بَرْزَخًا وَحِجْرًا مَّحْجُورًا

[Surah 25: Verse 53]

Chapter 13
Two More Observations

﴿٢٩﴾ أَلَمْ تَرَ أَنَّ اللَّهَ يُولِجُ اللَّيْلَ فِي النَّهَارِ وَيُولِجُ النَّهَارَ فِي اللَّيْلِ وَسَخَّرَ الشَّمْسَ وَالْقَمَرَ كُلٌّ يَجْرِي إِلَىٰ أَجَلٍ مُسَمًّى وَأَنَّ اللَّهَ بِمَا تَعْمَلُونَ خَبِيرٌ

[Surah 31: Verse 29]

﴿٥﴾ خَلَقَ السَّمَاوَاتِ وَالْأَرْضَ بِالْحَقِّ يُكَوِّرُ اللَّيْلَ عَلَى النَّهَارِ وَيُكَوِّرُ النَّهَارَ عَلَى اللَّيْلِ وَسَخَّرَ الشَّمْسَ وَالْقَمَرَ كُلٌّ يَجْرِي لِأَجَلٍ مُسَمًّى أَلَا هُوَ الْعَزِيزُ الْغَفَّارُ

[Surah 39: Verse 5]

﴿٣٣﴾ وَهُوَ الَّذِي خَلَقَ اللَّيْلَ وَالنَّهَارَ وَالشَّمْسَ وَالْقَمَرَ كُلٌّ فِي فَلَكٍ يَسْبَحُونَ

[Surah 21: Verse 33]

First Edition
(1426AH/2005AC)

© Copyright 1426AH/2005AC
amana publications
10710 Tucker Street
Beltsville, Maryland 20705-2223 USA
Tel: (301) 595-5999 / Fax: (301) 595-5888
E-mail: amana@igprinting.com
Website: www.amana-publications.com

Library of Congress Cataloging-in-Publication Data

Ashouri, Sami.
  Is the Qur'an God's word? : a scientific approach / Sami Ashouri.-- 1st ed..
    p. cm.
  Includes bibliographical references.
  ISBN 1-59008-035-1
  1. Koran and science. 2. Koran--Evidences, authority, etc. I. Title.

BP134.S3A85 2005
297.1'221--dc22
                              2005019705

Printed in Mexico by International Graphics
10710 Tucker Street, Beltsville, Maryland 20705-2223
Tel: (301) 595-5999 Fax: (301) 595-5888

Website: igprinting.com
E-mail: ig@igprinting.com

Is The Qur'an God's Word?
A Scientific Approach